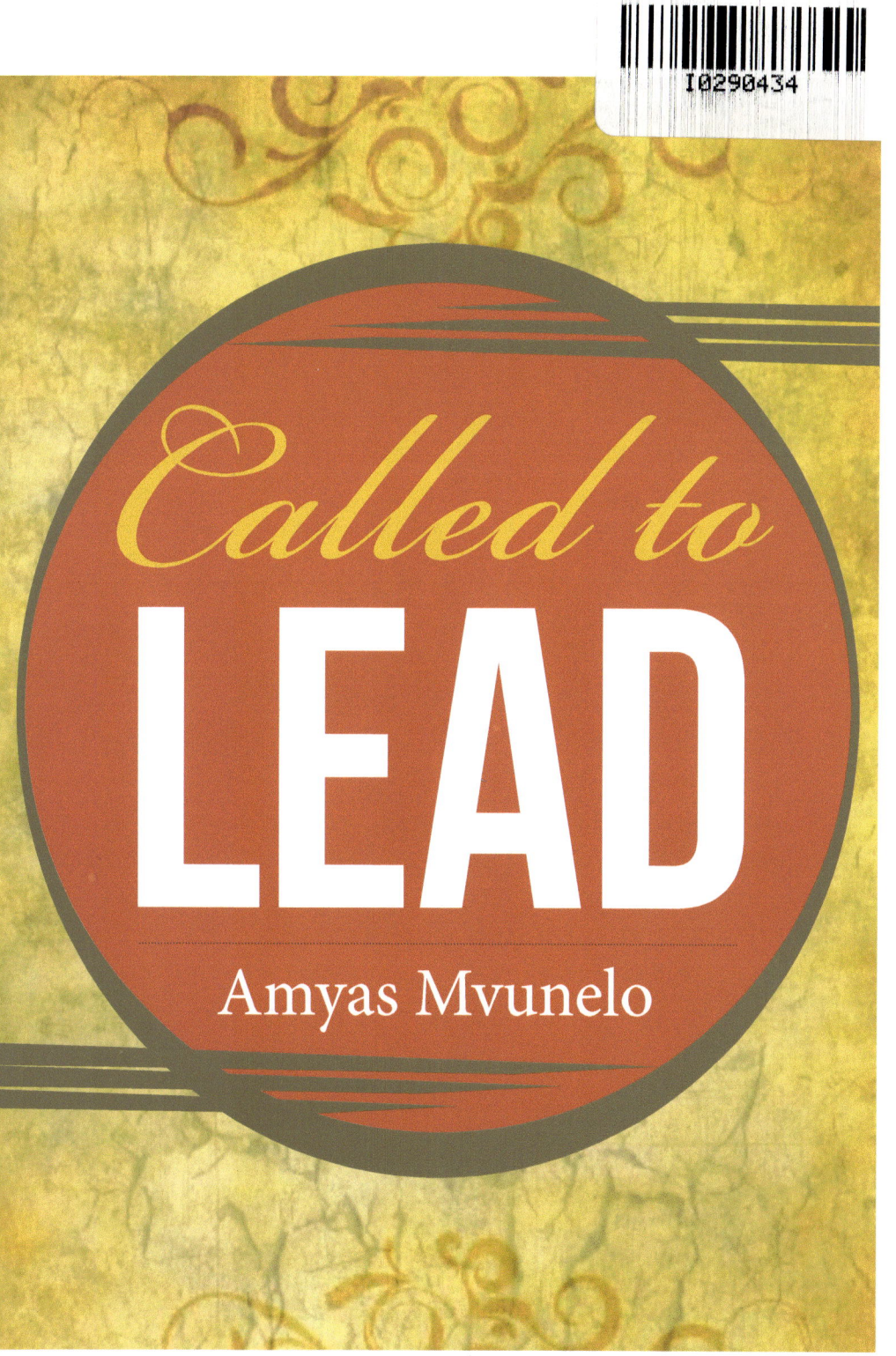

A LEADERSHIP TO THE POWER 7 SERIES BOOK

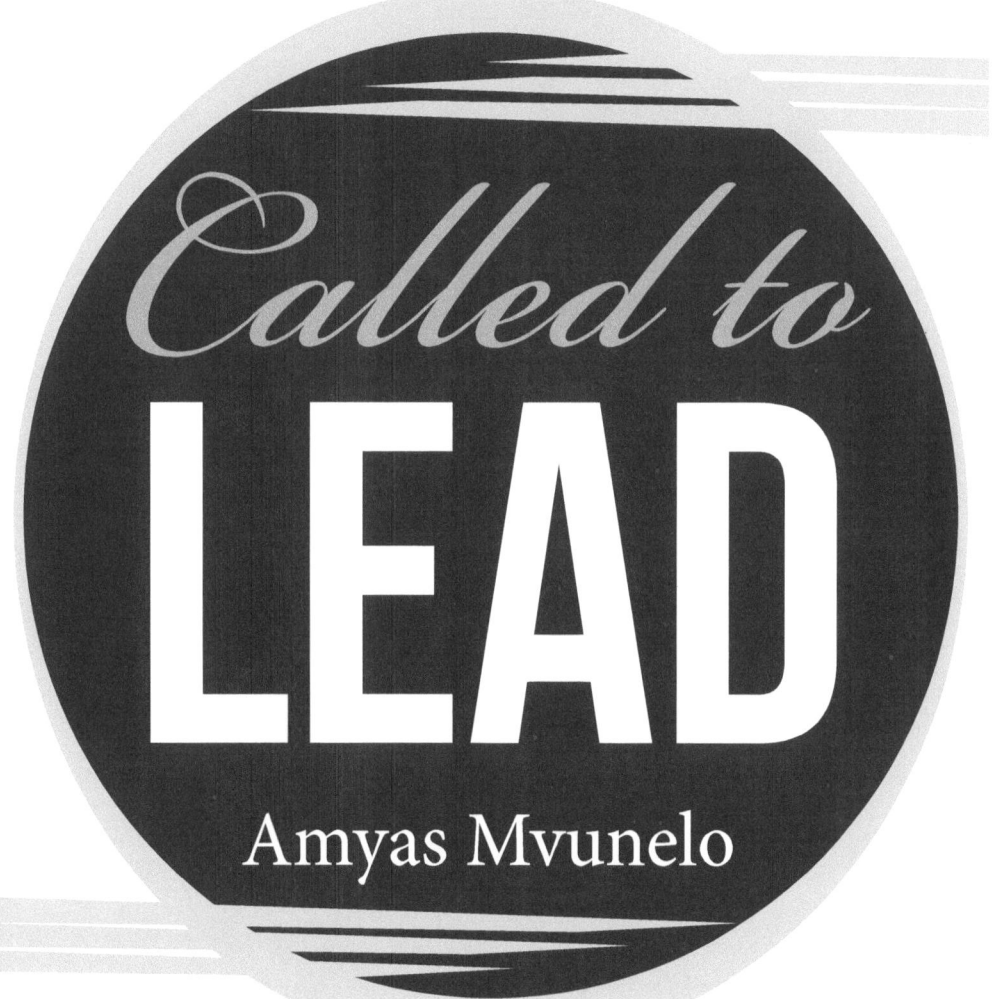

Published by

LEADA Media
a division of Leadership Education and Development Alliance,
a non-profit ministry with a mission to train, reskill, inspire, resource,
support, mentor, and transform Christians for effective leadership
contribution in business, politics, church, at home
and everywhere they are placed.

Printed and published in South Africa

Copyright © 2008, 2009 Amyas Mvunelo

Amyas Mvunelo hereby asserts his right to be
identified as the author of this work.

No part of this book may be reproduced, stored, in retrieval system
or transmitted in any form or by any means, electronic, mechanical,
photocopying, recording or otherwise, without the prior written permission
of the copyright owners.

Any content, views, or opinions presented in this book are solely those of
the author and do not necessarily represent those of his previous, present or
future employers.

All Scripture quotations, unless otherwise indicated, are
taken from The Message
Copyright © 1993, 1994, 1995, 1996, 2000, 2001, 2002, 2002
Used by permission of NavPress Publishing Group.

International edition ISBN 978-0-620-43537-6
Hard cover edition ISBN 978-0-620-41470-8

DEDICATION

To my wife, Bongiwe, who supports me in all my work and provides family leadership while I itinerate.

To my children, who test and reveal my leadership gaps and afford me an opportunity for leadership experimentation.

To Mfanelo & Nomasabatha Mbenenge for the risky investment in a stranger who claimed to be called.

ACKNOWLEDGEMENTS

PROJECT CONCEPTUALISER, INITIATOR & SUSTAINER:
God the Father, Jesus Christ & the Holy Spirit
Thank You for leadership opportunities, stamina and insights.

EDITORS:
Deirdre Colley, Ivy Peterson
Rebecca Joubert, Heather Tredoux

CONTRIBUTING REVIEWERS:
Jongimpi Papu, Mandla Lupondwana, Vincent Injetty, Mziyanda Mpiyane,
Donovan Stuurman, Monwabisi Kete, Eltie Links, Mfundo Mabenge.

PROOF READER:
Aevia Lupondwana

Thank you each one,
Amyas Mvunelo

ABOUT THE BOOK

Called to Lead is about leadership. The author, asserts that in as much as all must be followers, God has called and equipped every person to lead in some aspect of life. Some provide leadership, according to their sensed or distinct calling or placement, at home, at school, in the community, in church, in business, politics, education, science, economics and so on.

Leadership is about bettering people's lives wherever your leadership vocation beckons, making a contribution, and leaving a legacy. Experience the hand of God in your life as a leader as he calls, transforms, prepares and challenges you to greater heights in your leadership vocation.

While the book is written from a Christian perspective, it articulates broad based leadership praxis, and its principles are useful and applicable irrespective of one's occupation or station in life. As you are called, please lead!

ABOUT THE AUTHOR

Creative and innovative, a pioneer, a change agent, a pastor, poet, international public speaker and presenter, motivator and trainer, Amyas Mvunelo is both a practitioner and theorist in Christian Leadership.

Born and raised in South Africa's Eastern Cape, a province that has produced remarkable and courageous leadership personalities such as Steve Biko, Chris Hani, Nelson Mandela and the likes, he spent some time in voluntary exile in Botswana and came home as the new dispensation was being negotiated in his country of birth. With a degree in Theology from Andrews University in Michigan, USA, and a diploma in computer studies, as well as training in management, he entered pastoral ministry and soon gravitated to leadership development, a passion he pursues through research, writing and training.

Serving as a pastor in the Eastern Cape and Western Cape and later as the Regional Director of the Western Cape region, further gave him numerous opportunities to train many leaders of diverse backgrounds, persuasions and levels. Amyas and his wife, Bongiwe, together with their children, love reading, creating things, poetry, travelling, hosting and building cross cultural friendships.

Contents

Foreword 11
Introduction 12
Leadership Definitions.. 14

- **ESSENTIALS OF LEADERSHIP**

#1 Leadership is Vocational 21
#2 Leadership is Visionary 26
#3 Leadership is Relational... 31
#4 Leadership is Influence.. 35
#5 Leadership is Directing.. 37
#6 Leadership is Inspiring 40
#7 Leadership is Following God's Agenda 44

- **LEADERSHIP REALITIES**

#1 God Calls.. 49
#2 God Transforms 60
#3 God Prepares 73
#4 God Empowers 84
#5 God Sharpens 101
#6 God Replaces 116
#7 God Rewards... 127

- **LEADERSHIP VALUES**

#1 Honesty and Trustworthiness.. 131
#2 Justice and Fairness.. 134
#3 Responsibility and Accountability 137

Contents

#4 Integrity and Commitment 140
#5 Consistency and Goodness 143
#6 Transparency and Openness 145
#7 Self-Sacrificing Service 148

Called to Lead 151
Novice Prayer† 152
Apprentice Prayer† 152
Journeyman Prayer† 153
Master/Teacher Prayer† 153
Our High Calling 154
PRAYER FOR LEADERS 155
FURTHER READING 158

CALLED TO LEAD

Foreword

WELCOME TO LEADERSHIP TO THE POWER 7 SERIES!

The book you hold in your hands was born out my interest, passion and involvement with leadership education and development. I present it to you as both a dream come true and a dream-to-come-true project. I have had numerous opportunities to train and give presentations to leaders of varying backgrounds, cultures, organisational levels and persuasions, and have been inspired and enriched by the interaction.

To some extent this book is a mirror of my experience, observation and struggle with Christian leadership as well as my encouragement to those who take the time to lead.

I have come to appreciate the number seven as an icon of divine completeness, not finality, and have structured the book around seven for that reason. It is my hope that the seven points in each section will inspire you to endless possibilities as you pursue your leadership vocation.

May your leadership experience and growth be to the power seven - progressive completeness in God!

Introduction

1. Leadership is a complex interactive social engagement that has been subjected to definitions, theories, research, writing, speeches and dialogue.

At times, it has been confused with management and administration practice. For too long Christian leadership has been suffocating under the imported secular and sometimes dehumanising leadership theories.

The voice of Christian leadership has been unheard and shut out, until recently when even the marketplace and business literature has become dominated by the concept of Servant Leadership which emphasises Jesus as the Model Leader.

2. There are as many definitions of leadership as there are people who have thought, spoken, debated or written about this complex subject. Any definition reveals the definer's perspective and experience of leadership.

Unfortunately, definitions describe and articulate realities for those who read or listen. They affect people's thoughts on a particular subject; they also define reality as the people begin to apply, contextualise or fit themselves or reality to these theoretical statements.

3. I would like to suggest a definition of leadership that reflects my Christian understanding, thinking and worldview. It expresses both my perspective and ideals at the same time.

It may be correct to perceive it as a reaction to current views, trends and practices in leadership in both our world and in religious circles.

However, I am of the opinion that if understood and correctly applied, the leadership praxis I propose will be beneficial to those in religious circles as well as business persons and much more to those who straddle both realms.

4. You oftentimes hear an argument that suggests we should run the church like a business. If we acceded to that notion, I believe, as we see daily, we would have havoc, abuse and confusion because the bottom lines are not the same.

The simple reason is that leadership as currently practiced in the world of business and politics, seems to be more concerned with the bottom line, as in profits, and with leadership status, privilege, position, title and perks.

Our concept of leadership and success is evolutionary and survivalistic in both theory and practice. People are just a means to a classy lifestyle, comfortable office space and luxurious cars, and huge company profits.

In Christian leadership, both in theory and in practice, we should be more concerned about people than commercial gains. Sure, there's a lot we can learn from other spheres of life but we must be careful not to learn and adopt that which contradicts the biblical worldview and instruction.

5. My observation is that the abuse of both power and persons we too often see in Christian leadership is the result of applying secular leadership principles without considering the biblical worldview.

The treatment of the people by those who lead results into a survivalist organisational culture. It was Jesus, our Great Leader, who cautioned us against copying, imitating and integrating worldly practices into the Christian ethos.

6. To some extent, a Christian entrepreneur and an enterprise leader who is a Christian seems to be left with a choice to be a Christian at home and a crude business person between office hours.

As he or she takes off his or her jacket on Monday morning, it is as though Christianity is now stripped off, revealing a ferocious, survivalist business person whose thoughts, disposition, style, ethics, attitudes, interaction, reaction and decision making is simply about maximum profits with minimum input. This schizophrenic living turns the sweet and loving Christian of the weekend into a terrorising boss during the week.

7. Many are not just frustrated with the leadership praxis that not only dehumanises their fellow human beings but undermines their Christian faith and witness. We propose a different understanding and approach to leadership.

Leadership Definitions

1. "Leadership is the capacity and the will to rally men and women to a common purpose, and the character that inspires confidence," Bernard Montgomery.

Yes, leadership must be able to inspire confidence.

2. "A leader is a man [person] who knows the road, who can keep ahead and who can pull others after him," John R Mott.

A leader must be able to draw others towards his or her vision.

3. "A leader is a person who has the ability to get others to do what they don't want to do – and like it," Harry Truman.

Definitely, a leader must be able to seek and secure the cooperation and willingness of others, especially those he or she leads. People must come to a point where they adopt the leaders' vision as their own.

4. "Leadership occurs when one person induces others to work towards some predetermined objectives," Massie.

Leadership must indeed have a well thought-out vision, strategy, goals and

> "Leadership is action, not a position."
> ~ H. McGannon

"Leadership is the vocational, visionary and relational ability to influence, direct and inspire people towards God's agenda for their lives."
~ Amyas Mvunelo

VOCATIONAL
VISIONARY
RELATIONAL
INFLUENCE
DIRECTING
INSPIRING
GOD'S AGENDA

objectives in order for it to be mutually meaningful for those in the leadership engagement.

5. "If your actions inspire others to dream more, learn more, do more and become more, you are a leader," John Quincy Adams.

Successful leadership must not just inspire people to aspire but equally perspire towards great outcomes.

6. "Leadership is the art of influencing and directing people in a way that will win their obedience, confidence, respect and loyal cooperation in achieving common objectives," US Air Force.

Isn't it interesting that the US Air Force does not associate the use of force or commands with leadership? Those who have power, force and hierarchical authority think that leadership is influencing and directing people so as to win the obedience, confidence, respect and loyal cooperation of their subordinates.

7. I would like to suggest a leadership definition that we can carry all around wherever we are and whatever we do for a living.

Leadership is the vocational, visionary, and relational ability to influence, direct and inspire people towards the realisation of God's agenda.

Leaders are people who have accepted the vocation to provide vision and direction to their families, communities, organisations, enterprises and nations using their relational skills to influence, direct and inspire people towards the realisation of God's agenda for their lives.

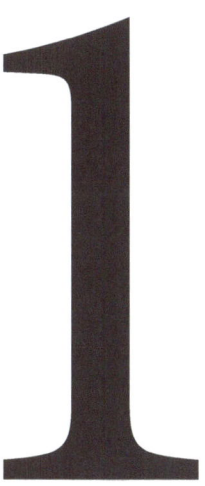

ESSENTIALS OF LEADERSHIP

*"All of the great leaders have had one
characteristic in common; it was the willingness to
confront unequivocally the major anxiety
of their people in their time. This, and not much
else, is the essence of leadership."
~ John Kenneth Galbraith ~*

ESSENTIAL #1 Leadership is Vocational

1. Vocation must be understood in this context as an inner urge, inclination or sense of being called, inspired by God, to follow, pursue or undertake a particular work, career, profession, occupation or cause in life, contributing towards the betterment of our world, and applicable to all people irrespective of their conscious or practised religious awareness.

2. Leadership is vocational in that it is a calling from God to all humanity. God calls persons to lead in some aspect of life, to the benefit of all or immediate humanity. We do not quite understand how it comes about except we realise it in men and women throughout history and in our personal lives.

Some have suggested that leadership is a special ability that some are born with, observing that it comes naturally and spontaneously to some without any prior leadership education and training.

The argument has caused leadership to be thought of and perceived as the terrain of the chosen or privileged elite, and that the rest are just destined to be followers. I would like to suggest that leadership is a gift and competence of all people under the sun. It is an inherent capacity, mandate and directive given to humanity after creation.

With some people leadership shows itself prominently while with others it may be latent, undeveloped, underdeveloped and unrealised yet. John Maxwell is right when he says "After creating the universe and the planet on which we live, He handed leadership of the earth over to humankind," (Maxwell 2007).

Our greatest challenge which has led to the dearth of true leadership is that we are not cognisant and intentional about leadership in our thinking and practice; we want to leave it to a few who have realised and embraced its relevance and use for their lives and benefit of others.

"The truth is that few people are naturals when it comes to leading others. But everyone has potential... Sociologists say that even introverted people will influence an average of 10,000 people in their lifetime... Someone who is not even trying to lead others will impact many," (ibid).

3. While with others the leadership gift comes naturally and effortlessly, some have to unmask it the hard way of training, trial and error, practice, experience, and deliberate, calculated and conscious development. Personal circumstances may play a major role.

The extent to which parents, siblings, peers, educators and social formations in the formative years allow and encourage children to take courageous initiative, make discretionary decisions, use risky innovations and redefine reality (breaking and reshaping toys, for an example), frees or inhibits the spontaneous development of leadership potential.

But all have in their arsenal leadership versatility that must be discovered, developed, used and advanced for the betterment of other people's lives. To say that leadership is natural or acquired is not to say that God is not involved in both the giving of the ability as well as in the unearthing or pruning processes.

4. To lead in any sphere is to accept God's purpose for humanity and a divine call whether or not the leader recognises and treats it as such. Over the years we have come to narrow God's calling to such professions as being a pastor, teacher, and nurse and lately we have confined it exclusively to pastoral ministry.

God, throughout Scripture, has called leaders to make various leadership contributions. There are numerous scriptural examples of calls to various people to provide family, community, political, religious, educational, business and project leadership.

It is not God who has stopped calling people but we have lessened our understanding of vocation to spiritual calling and technical training.

I believe that all who lead in politics and public life, business and economics, science and education, health and welfare, arts and culture, technology and in the intellectual enterprises and all spheres of positive human living, are equally called as those who serve in the religious domain.

Often times, however, we have people who use their leadership calling and abilities for selfish ends. Some of the leaders use their leadership gifts to the disadvantage of the very people that God intended to be blessed by the leader.

We have the likes of Adolf Hitler and the architects of apartheid whose

> All of us must follow our leadership calling
> whatever we sense, discover or realise
> it to be to the honour and glory of our Maker
> and Caller, and to the benefit and
> advancement of God-created humanity.

capabilities could have benefited our world, going down in history as the worst nightmares from which we are still struggling to wake up.

5. All of us must follow our leadership calling whatever we sense, discover or realise it to be and do it to the honour and glory of our Maker and Caller and to the benefit and advancement of God-created humanity, irrespective of our or people's station, status, lifestyle, health condition, culture, religion, nationality, race or gender. We are called to put smiles around people's faces, not frowns, sorrow and misery.

6. Each one of us has been called to provide leadership and be led in some aspect of life and this vocation shall last as long as our life shall last. It is to be a lifelong occupation. We shall not be released from leadership until God who is the Caller shall let us rest.

The leadership vocation may have a number of vehicles through which it is driven and revealed. It may be through positions, titles or nothing at all. Even though there may be temporal or position related opportunities of leadership, a leader is a leader for life.

A developed leader will be ever ready to lead, regardless of the position he or she is elected to occupy or an opportunity or gap or lack thereof.

Great leaders do not need positions to lead. True leadership does not depend on position or title to lead and influence people. Sometimes, the more influential people are not those who occupy elective positions, it is ordinary men and women whose names are not prefixed or sandwiched with any fancy titles.

7. Finally, we are accountable to God on how we use our sensed calling and how

we benefit others with our vocation, accompanying abilities, gifts and skills, opportunities and privileges.

We are accountable to Him and others even now as His stewards but ultimately at the end of time when we shall have to give account at the judgement.

We do not always know where God intends to ultimately employ us, or where life shall lead us to. We must learn to take every leadership opportunity that we have now or in the future as a 'God-given invitational' to prepare for greater leadership contribution.

We may consider our disadvantages to be the worst but in the end it may turn out to be the best for us personally as well as for the beneficiaries of our leadership. Daniel was thrust out of his familiar zone to a foreign land.

He could have been miserable under those hostile circumstances. That situation in the end worked out to be God's vehicle of not only empowering him for his outstanding leadership vocation but also blessed Babylon and the entire world through his prophetic interpretation, prophetic contribution and illustrious career as a civil servant.

ESSENTIAL #2 Leadership is Visionary

1. Theodore Hesburg is right when he observed; "The very essence of leadership is that you have to have a vision." Leaders by definition are visionaries, those who see different realities beyond the visible, beyond what appears to be established as normal and final.

2. The reason humanity and life are significantly different from the past is, to a large extent, attributable to leadership dreams and visions – visionary leadership catching sight of what we have today before it becomes part of us.

Though humanity has been persistently slow and stubborn to hear and respond to the echoes of the future beckoning us to greater heights every day, God has continued to inspire those who are willing to boldly redefine reality, towards the approximation of the divine ideals for humanity, albeit not without resistance and stoning from their peers and contemporaries.

> "The future belongs to those who see possibilities before they become obvious."
> ~ John Sculley ~

3. Visionaries or great leaders catch mental pictures of new reality derived from God's purposive movements and activity on earth. They catch a glimpse of an end that is slightly or totally different from the existing one and dare to dream, wake up, labour and inspire others towards the realisation of that new reality, engaging both individual energy, team and group synergy.

4. Great leaders or visionaries transcend the present realities and see beyond the dust and rut of daily life to worlds unknown, past the apparently insurmountable mountains that stand between the conceived potentiality and realised actuality, taking calculated risks towards the realisation of the dream.

Sadly though, there are many dreams that have been miscarried, aborted, and have expired and are buried in the graves because some dreamers go back to sleep after they have been given the vision or dream.

CALLED TO LEAD

> "Great spirits have always found violent opposition from mediocrities. The latter cannot understand it when a man does not thoughtlessly submit to hereditary prejudices but honestly and courageously uses his intelligence."
> ~ Albert Einstein ~

Some look at the cost to be paid and weigh their life too precious to be martyrs of the God given dream. Others dare not rock the boat, while others refuse to see the vision shown and choose to complacently defend the historical reality as God's final say and reality for humanity.

5. A visionary or leader is someone who lives with us yet sees beyond us. He or she dwells among us as one of us but asks different questions than most of us care or dare to ask. He or she looks at our mundane routines and restlessly asks whether or not we have arrived at the pinnacle of intended living.

A visionary stands on the summit and casts reflective eyes across infinity and sees a tunnel of possibilities shining its light through our apparently complete realities.

When the visionaries grasp unimagined, unseen and unheard of realities, they pen it down in their hearts and return to the realities that now appear gloomy and hopeless, and brave visionaries refuse to remain the same or silent.

They perceive the magnitude of the contrast between what they have seen on the summit of dreams and what they see in their valley of business as usual. They gradually begin to reconcile the two and soon realise that new wine cannot be contained in old wine skins, a paradigm shift must occur in the face of ordinary achievements.

Visionaries, carrying the images of new reality, not only inspire other towards the change but begin to be agents of change.

6. Any leader who has caught any vision needs courage as a shield because those who have not seen what he or she has seen on the mountaintop will disparage and distract by sneering at any deviation from the norm, insisting that the present or past formulas are better than the futuristic alternatives or the challenges are insurmountable and the status quo is an adequate definition of reality.

The visionary, the affected and resistant must remember that what is now accepted as normal and traditional was unimagined and non-existent at some stage but gradually became a formation of tried recipes of reality because some visionary, or a number of them at some stage imagined, envisioned and established the new reality as a way of life, a way of doing life, doing church, doing politics, science, technology and business.

Of course, this is not license to do as one pleases; changing for the sake of change, but when time to change has come those who are receptive and adaptable to change, will survive. We must change for progress or betterment.

Unfortunately, the resistant will either be reactionaries or attempt to do away with their revolutionary counterparts. But the revolutionary must relentlessly pursue what he or she has seen on the mountaintop.

History reveals the fate of the reactionaries, traditionalists, and conservatives; those who stand in the way of change and revolutions – they disappear into oblivion and a new reality is established for future generations, notwithstanding their resistance or disbelief.

7. To lead indeed is to yield, listening to God again and again, consulting with and hearing the people on whom your vision and leadership will have an impact. Any leader who is not willing to listen to either God or the people or both is not fit to lead. However, a leader should never stop, especially when criticised and when discouraging comments are made or the occasional criticism and suspicion.

Accelerate on in faith, hope and courage, weaving them as both ingredients and thirst quenchers en route to the realisation of the envisioned end. Some who doubt now may finally have their eyes opened.

Visionaries or great leaders catch mental pictures of new reality derived from God's purposive movements and activity on earth.

They catch a glimpse of an end that is slightly or totally different from the existing one and dare to dream, wake up, labour and inspire others towards the realisation of that new reality, engaging both individual energy, team and group synergy.

ESSENTIAL #3 Leadership is Relational

1. After being at the mountain top, having seen the Promised Land and having been transformed by the vision of the new realities, leaders must return to and connect with their people in a human and humane manner. "[You] must unite your constituents around a common (sic) cause and connect with them as human beings," says James Kouzes and Barry Posner.

2. Leaders, having caught the vision, return to their people and endeavour to influence and inspire them to leave their valleys of ordinariness, mediocrity and self-sufficiency, climb the mountain and rise up to the summit not just to imagine or catch a glimpse of that new reality but to come to terms with its beckoning, and enter its promise.

Leaders must relate to their people, dialogue with them and inspire their yearning for the realisation of the vision. Great leaders do not force their vision upon people. Great leaders do not command or force their people to follow them but through communication, relationships, mutual engagement and persuasive dialogue and inspiration, they enthuse their people to aspire towards the vision.

3. No one effectively influences or serves people while living in esoteric isolation and being understood by only a few people with specialised knowledge or intellect.

Through simple deliberate interactions, service and presence among the people, the leader is afforded an opportunity to infuse the vision in such a way that the people identify with and sometimes crystallise their leader's vision, and they adopt it as their own.

Only then do they allow themselves to be transformed by the leader's vision, when they can identify with its promise. According to Gilbert Amelio, "Developing excellent communication skills is absolutely essential to effective leadership." I always say leadership is 70% communication, and without communication in its various shades and styles, little will be accomplished.

The leader must be able to share knowledge and ideas to transmit a sense of

> **Leaders, having caught the vision, return to their people and endeavour to influence and inspire them to leave their valleys of ordinariness, mediocrity and self-sufficiency, climb the mountain and rise up to the summit not just to catch a glimpse of that new reality but to come to terms with its beckoning, and enter its promise.**

urgency and enthusiasm to others. If a leader can't get a message across clearly and motivate others to act on it, then having a message doesn't even matter. A leader articulates and crystalises the vision in understandable communication, based on the relationship the leader has build with the people he or she leads.

4. Great leaders realise that no amount of mountain beckoning, shouting, fear drumming or commanding voice will genuinely bring the people to the leader's vision, aspirations and intentions.

According to Michael A. Hogg, "Leadership is a relational term—it identifies a relationship in which some people are able to persuade others to adopt new values, attitudes and goals, and to exert effort on behalf of those values, attitudes and goals. The relationship is almost always configured by and played out within the parameters of a group—a small group like a team, a medium sized group like an organization, or a large group like a nation. The values, attitudes and goals that leaders inspire others to adopt and to follow are ones that define and serve the group—and thus leaders are able to transform individual action into group action."

5. The engaging and interactive leader then allows people to internalise and run with the vision, fueling it with more vigour than if the leader had not released it from his or her stable.

"A leader is best when people barely know he exists, when his work is done, his aim fulfilled, and they will say: 'We did it ourselves,'" Lao Tzu advises.

6. Great leaders are not afraid to relate to and with their people. Their people feel some connectedness and solidarity with their leader, so much so that an injury or setback to their leader or the vision is an injury to them personally.

Theodore Roosevelt remarked; "The most important single ingredient in the formula of success is knowing how to get along with people." This is the hardest yet essential aspect of leadership.

7. Christian leadership, unlike any other, is activated and supercharged by relationships and mutual connectedness of the leader and those who are being led. All leaders should make it their daily business to learn how to get along with people, even the most difficult people.

We must continually seek to understand human behaviour to understand people's pulse and tempo if we hope to lead people, and not machines, towards God's agenda for their lives.

We must learn to build sustainable and meaningful relationships with those we lead.

ESSENTIAL #4 Leadership is Influence

1. Christian leadership needs redemption from the use of force, power, manipulation, intimidation, threats, tricks, fear, authority and position as a means of bringing about obedience or change.

We must stay clear of bullying on the basis of leadership positions, age and cultural positioning. We must avoid militaristic tendencies and language as these create false obedience among the followers, while revealing arrogance and abusive power in leaders.

2. In order to reach or approximate the intended divine outcomes, God's methods must be used by Christian leaders, taking cues from the manner in which God deals with us as He leads us as sinners to His heights.

3. Although Christ has all power, and commands the universe, He has chosen persuasive love to influence us towards positive and voluntary change.

4. The method with which Christ has chosen to influence humanity is persuasive love rather than trying to intimidate by making grand and terrifying gestures and demands. God's method may appear to have a slow effect, yet the results are eternally thorough. Force, intimidation, drumming of fear and manipulation may seem to bring results immediately, but the damage may be eternal.

5. Christ, our Leader, could have used forceful and militaristic means to bring about change in the disciples and those He sought to convert, but He has allowed his influence to outlive Him as a life-changing legacy to this day.

6. To see genuine transformation requires that we step out of the way and let God lead through us, while we patiently do whatever we need to do to influence others to see God through our lives, even through our struggles.

7. Our way is to lead through influence and example. By calming, harnessing, nurturing and harmonising the inner and public person, trimming and pruning as we go along, until we reach alignment and compatibility with the divine nature, and we are able to infuse divine ideals by our lifestyle and through our leadership. Of course, this is incompatible with human nature.

"Everyone comes between men's souls and God, either as a brick wall or as a bridge. Either you are leading men to God or you are driving them away."
~ Lindsay Dewar ~

ESSENTIAL #5 Leadership is Directing

1. A sense of direction is important. It determines where you walk to get to where you want to be in the end.

2. We direct people towards a particular direction that we either know experientially or have experienced second-hand. Either way, we must be clear, very clear, about the direction, so that we can give direction, or we will fumble and misdirect others.

3. To be effective in Christian leadership we must be able to give directions to people. Like the sons of Issachar, we must understand the times and know what must be done (1 Chron 12:32). According to James Kouzes and Barry Posner, "There's nothing more demoralising than a leader who can't clearly articulate why we're doing what we're doing."

4. Our direction is derived from both our sense and impression of our vocation and vision - what you have heard and seen during the mountain-top experience - and that map must be carried at all times to give direction to your course, cause and contribution.

5. You may lose your direction, but if you continually refresh your energies with your sense of direction, your compass, you will always work and fall closer to where you intended to reach when you started off in your leadership course.

6. Many times, being without a vision and being directionless keeps us walking too long with little or no care where we land, or with whom we end up.

7. Leaders must regularly and frequently clarify and articulate their vision to give direction to the followers; reminding the people of the dream that must be pursued or else the many crowds following them will be lost in wonderland.

The Obamas of our time must stand again and again, as they did before, and must not retreat or bury themselves or their inspiring vision in mundane demands of business.

> Would you tell me, please, which way I ought to go from here?"
> "That depends a great deal on where you want to get to," said the Cat.
> "I don't much care where—"said Alice. "Then it doesn't much matter which way you go," said the Cat. "—so long as I get somewhere," Alice added as an explanation.
> "Oh, you're sure to do that," said the Cat, "if only you walk long enough."
> ~ Lewis Carroll ~

They must continually echo hope and assurances to the disillusioned multitudes; they must repeatedly speak of the possibility of overcoming the hardships that confront us and they must give direction to the masses whose confidence in their leaders' dreams and themselves are dying in their leaders' increasing and worrisome silence.

With little or no direction, our glimpse of hope fades away and our sense of direction will be lost and we will be left wondering in the desert of despair and disorientation longer than 40 years.

Leaders must continually give direction and inspiration to their constituencies, otherwise the followers may direct themselves to places that will be difficult for the leader to call them back from, after a long time.

ESSENTIAL #6 Leadership is Inspiring

1. No leader has seen the realisation of his vision without a need to encourage those who follow behind and those who walk ahead so that they all stay on course.

2. The road up the Mountain of Life is full of dangers and pitfalls. Many stumble and fall, or get trapped and bruised, but a leader's encouraging words will inspire a wounded soldier's heart back to life faster than an unfamiliar doctor's touch.

3. Robert Louis Stevenson's advice is true but incomplete when he says: "Keep your fears to yourself, but share your inspiration with others." Leaders' wells run dry too and their thirsting souls need refreshing in the desert of life.

4. A leader also needs inspiration and encouragement at some stage. Practise broadcasting your fears and perplexities in the audience of God, and whisper them to your close family and friends.

Refresh your soul in tearful conversations with God and receive renewal at the well of agonising faith. In their book, *Lead Like Jesus,* Ken Blanchard and Phil Hodges say;

"Leadership can be a lonely business filled with great amounts of soul-draining human interaction but little soul-filling intimacy. Without some safe-harbour relationships where we can only lay down all the armor and weapons needed to face the world and relax in confidence and unguarded communion, we become vulnerable to two debilitating frames of mind and spirit – the victim and the martyr," (Blanchard & Hodges 2005).

5. Take heart in this; all of God's leaders are born in difficulty, trained in trying circumstances, graduated in tribulation, so that they are able to encourage, inspire and strengthen people.

Better a leader who knows what it is to fail than a leader who will be intolerant of other people's misstep, and who, in the failure to understand the need of the mistaken team mate, might dismiss potential prematurely.

6. In all you do, develop the gift of discernment or emotional intelligence to see the weeping hearts of the people you lead; otherwise you will be thought of as an insensitive and uninspiring technocrat.

Many leaders are not aware of the needs, feelings and joys of the people they lead and they go past their people in their busyness with the targets, programmes and achievements.

Take the time to inspire your team to see why they do what they have to do.

Inspiration is challenging your people to greater heights and infusing a desirable vision in the minds of your people, and it is keeping that vision, with forceful words and powerful imagery, before their eyes, in such a way that they all strive towards its realisation.

Great leaders know that people have short memory and he or she has to repeatedly rejuvenate people with gripping inspiration and hope in such a way that those who may be stricken with amnesia, fatigue and laziness may continually rise up to the challenge and be the carriers and executors of the desired outcome.

Other leaders ignore their people's cries and need for inspiration but hope for great results by their singular sweating in the projects that must be completed.

The task of leadership is to envision the desired end, articulate the vision to as many as need to hear it, inspire and galvanise the team and constituencies to work towards the vision's fulfillment, modeling the values, culture and behaviour for the team, mobilising resources and means to bring the vision to its feet, mentor and support the foot soldiers, and monitoring and evaluating progress made.

Inspiration becomes an essential lubricant of the shared vision and it is imperative that leaders learn to listen to the heartbeat of the people they lead in order to be effective in their leadership.

Leaders must be familiar with their people's struggle in the same way they need to be familiar with the vision they seek to realise.

7. Finally, leaders must learn the art of encouraging and praying in such a way that the giants of fear and discouragements shrink in the face of faith. It may

CALLED TO LEAD

> The Obamas of our time must stand again and again, as they did before, and must not retreat or bury themselves or their inspiring vision in mundane demands of business. They must continually echo hope and assurances to the disillusioned multitudes; they must repeatedly speak of the possibility of overcoming the hardships that confront us and they must give direction to the masses whose confidence in their leaders' dreams and themselves are dying in their leaders' increasing and worrisome silence. With little or no direction, our glimpse of hope fades away and our sense of direction will be lost and we will be left wondering in the desert of despair and disorientation longer than 40 years.

take a few minutes of the leader's time to be there when their people need them most.

Sometimes, without spoken words, a leader's presence may inspire the people and team he or she leads. That you called, or came at the time of need, will inspire your people.

Keep your vanguard motivated all the time as low morale has an effect on team performance.

ESSENTIAL #7 Leadership is Following God's Agenda

1. Other leaders lead towards predetermined common goals, but for Christian leaders God has unilaterally set the agenda that a Christian must follow before calling together the leadership personnel. Every leader must first be a follower or disciple of Jesus in order to lead towards God and His agenda for His people.

2. We are all guests called to a banquet with a menu determined for us, and we have not been mandated to change it. We are participants in the historic and prophetic continuum; making our mark as did our forebears, passing the torch to the next generation to carry forward.

3. In God's kingdom we have to do things on God's terms and ethics to arrive at His ends in His time. Christian leaders follow God's agenda for their own lives and the lives of those they lead. We must lead people not to our own target, selfish ambitions or our preferred style or mode of leadership.

Christian leadership must always begin with a number of questions such as "What is God's purpose for entrusting us to lead." The other question, again asked from God, is "How should we lead?"

It is impossible to force people to a particular direction or to dictate to them how and what they should do, and then conclude that God wanted us to force them.

God's agenda is not achieved by use of strange fires such as force, misinformation, exploitation, deception and so on.

4. We must also continually and deliberately resist the temptation of presenting ourselves as the agenda or forwarding our own items to be pursued. God's agenda is eternal, fair and transparent, and ours is temporal, unfair, manipulative, limited, selfish and hidden.

5. God's agenda for the world is Salvation and Service – our saving and caring relationship with Him and with one another. God intended that humanity

> **We must also continually and deliberately resist the temptation to forward ourselves as the agenda or forward our own items to be pursued.**

should find fulfillment in relating to Him who is the Source and Sustainer of life. In Him we are complete and regain our life in abundance.

We also relate to one another and the rest of creation because we are at peace with Him. We find rest for our troubled souls and are at peace with our surroundings and our neighbour.

In the Garden of Eden, we broke that essential connection with God and began to resemble that with which we associated. When we began to think of ourselves as akin to apes, we began to behave like or worse than they do. Salvation is God's hand stretched out around our earth, reaching out to us through the Cross of Jesus, calling us back to the Father's bosom, back to His agenda.

6. As we respond to Love, we love what He loves, and we turn to each other in familial love, and find joy and fulfillment in serving each other selflessly. This is God's programme; this is our calling – to become one another's caregivers, lifting our arms to help another person in need.

Let us lift our arms in loving and serving embraces, not in destructive and dehumanising war.

7. Our measure of performance is set strictly in terms of God's agenda and we must fail or succeed in this, nothing else.

We are creatures of love and love fulfills us. Love completes and humanises our hearts of stone. Love stops wars, hatred, bitterness and hopelessness.

CALLED TO LEAD

LEADERSHIP REALITIES
The Truths about Leadership

*"How you choose to respond each moment
to the movie of life determines how you see the next
frame, and the next, and eventually
how you feel when the movie ends."*
~ Doc Childre ~

REALITY #1 God Calls

Leadership is God's original plan for humanity

1. God created humanity with leadership capabilities, authority, a mandate and God himself as the model. "After creating the universe and the planet on which we live, He handed leadership of the earth over to humankind (Gen 1:2)," observed John Maxwell.

2. "You and I were created to lead and to rule. Sin marred our ability to lead," Maxwell observed.

3. Salvation seeks to restore the original intentions of God for humanity, and that includes leadership as part of the restoration package.

4. We are called to be partners or "co-workers" with God in all His work. God is inspiring leaders everywhere in our world to be His Hands, to put a smile on some person's face.

5. We have been mandated and delegated by the Great Leader to lead His people to His ideals and, even though sin attempted to disrupt God's plans, we are still called to lead God's people according to His agenda over the sin hurdle.

6. Leadership qualities have been evident in humanity from creation, albeit distorted and misguided at times. We must recognise them, acknowledge them, and embrace them as God's gift to humanity in the past, present and in the future.

7. It is through good leadership that the world has come this far, and it is through great leadership that the world will advance further. True leadership, following God's Call, does not leave our world the same, it changes it for the better, aligning itself towards God's original purpose for humanity.

CALLED TO LEAD

The leadership call comes at different stages in life and is lifelong

1. We may not hear or recognize it but God's call comes to us even before we are born. Jeremiah was reminded of his pre-birth calling to lead the nation's religious and prophetic ministry beyond the national borders (Jer 1:5).

2. Children also hear the voice of God calling them even though they do not always understand everything they may be responding to, as was the case when Samuel was called, (1 Sam 3:4).

3. David and many young people received God's call in their youthfulness, (1 Sam 16:13).

4. While busying himself with his unpopular job, already an adult with a family of his own, Matthew responds to a call not just to follow Jesus but to also play a leading role in God's mission, (Matt 9:9).

5. The call to leadership has no limitation on time and age. David's leadership vocation spanned his entire adult life. Our writing prophets such as Daniel who revealed the future of our world still prove helpful to us as we search for the meaning and purpose as well as the end of our living.

6. Great leaders may even be called to provide leadership in retirement, though to a lesser or a different degree. Again, Daniel, a retired civil servant, is called out of retirement to share his prophetic wisdom and intelligence.

Many leadership luminaries continue to influence us, even though they have retreated from public and active life.

7. In some instances a leader's legacy lives on beyond his life and death. Jesus is revered as a leader par excellence while His influence has not only seen millions of people over the generations becoming His disciples, the corporate world is now turning to Jesus as the epitome of good leadership.

More and more business leaders are adopting Robert K Greenleaf's Servant Leadership model as they realise that the "power-centered authoritarian leadership style" is not working and yielding the results hoped for – a culture of service and relationships.

In fact Greenleaf whose life spanned 86 years, of which only 20 of them were spent as a leadership theorist, has this credited to his legacy by Wikipedia; "Today there are scores of colleges and universities that include Servant Leadership in their teachings and hundreds of companies that embrace Greenleaf's philosophy. As Greenleaf strived to serve through education, he became the leader of a movement."

God's leadership call may be specific and local

1. God specifies the task that must be carried out by the leader or leaders whom He is calling.

Jesus' specific task included preaching, teaching, healing and dying for the redemption of the world that had gone astray and would have been forever lost.

2. Some leadership calls are time-related and they end at the specified or allowed time, and we never hear about them again.

3. Within the leadership call the specific local context to which the call applies may have no universal application or relevance. In other instances it may be glocal or may have global relevance.

4. Particulars of the intended beneficiaries are sometimes stated in the leadership call.

5. Partners, participants and role players are specified in some of these leadership calls.

6. The terms and conditions may be revealed as part of the call.

7. God has specific, desired outcomes for each leadership call. Each time God calls a person to leadership, there are specific outcomes that must be achieved.

God's call may be generic and global

1. God's call is sometimes generic enough to apply globally.

2. Sometimes it is generic enough to apply to all contexts, cultures and conditions.

3. Sometimes, though initially given with a particular and specific context or people, it applies universally.

4. In such instances, it's a call to all God's people globally to do something in the divinely ordained project, irrespective of their age, culture, race, circumstances, abilities, occupations, wealth or strengths.

5. Sometimes leadership applies individually and corporately, that is to say we must all do something about it as individuals, as families, as organisations, as communities as well as the Church.

6. Evangelism or welfare is such a leadership call. It is a call to all of us as God's people globally to lead souls to God and to take care of our economically disadvantaged people among us.

7. The methods will be adaptable to the people's context but the end will be the same – people will be led towards God's agenda for their lives.

God's call may be special and personal

1. Sometimes God calls leaders for a unique leadership contribution, adding new or revising existing knowledge, meaning, system, component, function, process or project.

2. At such times God impresses or speaks to the person called in a personal, particular and clear manner.

3. The person called, knows his special function or mission from the divine encounter and realises it as personal purpose either at the beginning, midstream or in the end.

4. Sometimes, especially when the person is reluctant or unsure, God manifests the call repeatedly and/or in various ways using the person's interest, passion, experience, inclination, and skills as a confirmation towards a particular project.

5. God does not expect blind or irrational acceptance of the call, although it may not always be clear to the person that they are actually following God's purpose for their lives. You will find that the call has always been there as you scrutinise your past and present.

6. Where a special call is sensed, heard or experienced, the onus to test the veracity of the call rests with the person called, as well as with the established community of faith, and people in his or her life who must honestly advise the person towards God's will rather than their wishes.

7. The Caller is kind enough to help earnest seekers through the verification process, and will provide evidence to assure you of His intentions.

Each is called for a special and unique contribution

1. Whatever your field or position, there are opportunities for that unique and special contribution. Each of us is a unique individual with unique experience and expertise, and God calls us to make unique contributions to His work, service and the upliftment of humanity.

2. The world must be different because you, a unique person with a unique personality, came with your unique experience, skills and competencies. Even though your leadership opportunity may be in the same areas as others, your contribution is for a specific purpose and a special contribution in that portfolio.

Though the four gospel writers wrote on one subject, they each made a special contribution guided by their uniqueness. Though God could have brought them together for the project to ensure uniformity, He allowed them to write in various ways, and we are enriched by their diversity.

3. While you learn from others, your predecessors and mentors, never try to replicate their special contribution, otherwise the world remains the same before and after you.

> "Each of us is meant to have a character all our own, to be what no other can exactly be, and do what no other can exactly do."
> ~ William Ellery Channing ~

A leader takes in all but makes the final decision. A good leader is not just a reflector of other people's ideas and thoughts but he or she thinks through every advice received and makes it his or her own.

Somebody said; "Don't follow any advice, no matter how good, until you feel as deeply in your spirit as you think in your mind that the counsel is wise."

No advisor or mentor should expect that all his or her suggestions and guidance will be implemented because it must go through the sieve of personal judgment and uniqueness of the advisee. James Callaghan cautions that a "leader must have the courage to act against an expert's advice."

4. Avoid competition and professional jealousy; rejoice with those who make a special mark, and quietly make your own without allowing 'the green-eyed monster' to ruin your enjoyment of life.

5. Increase your usefulness, sharpening the saw from time to time through reading, training or learning new skills.

6. Explore as many opportunities and possibilities as possible. However, know and use your areas of strength and compliment your limitations and lack through the team that God has surrounded you with.

7. Make yourself indispensable in terms of your special skills and contribution, but be dispensable regarding your attitude in your leadership assignment, ready to give way when called to. Make excellence and humility inseparable – unfortunately a rare find today among leaders.

It is through good leadership that the
world has come this far, and it is
through great leadership that the
world will advance further.

True leadership, following God's Call, does
not leave our world the same,
it changes it for the better.

Each is called and equipped for service to God and others

1. God has called us for His purposes, not for our own agenda or self-glorification.

2. We have not been called for self-interest but are fulfilled in serving and benefiting others. Do your duty to God and humanity, more so to the betterment of people, and their lives. Our duty is to God and to His creation, especially people whom He treasures most.

3. Christ came to serve and uplift humanity, and was prepared to die to reach that goal. This is what characterises and distinguishes true leadership – preparedness to suffer and die for the sake of the cause and for people. Leaders who have something to die and sacrifice for, if need be, have found meaning and something to live for.

4. While we do not apply to be martyrs, we must be prepared to suffer and die for God's sake and His cause, like the pioneers did.

5. As Christian leaders we are to consider personal convenience third in line to the service of God and humanity. "A leader is not an administrator who loves to run others, but someone who carries water for his people so that they can get on with their jobs," Robert Townsend.

6. The leader's prayer should be; "Teach us, Lord, to serve you as you deserve; To give and not count the cost; To fight and not heed the wounds; To toil and not seek for rest; To labour and not ask for any reward; Save that of knowing that we do Your will," Ignatius of Loyola said.

7. It is through good leadership that the world has come this far, and it is through great leadership that the world will advance further. True leadership, following God's Call, does not leave our world the same, it changes it for the better.

REALITY #2 God Transforms

Discipleship is primary and leadership is secondary

1. A Christian leader is a person who has accepted Jesus Christ and His way of life – a person of God. It is essential in Christian leadership that before becoming a person for God, one is a person of God. Be in discipleship first before being in leadership.

Discipleship is primary and leadership is secondary in Christian leadership, not the other way round. Often we flaunt our leadership abilities as evidence of our connection with Jesus. But character is evidence of discipleship not leadership.

All natural, acquired or spiritual gifts are not the fruit of the Spirit but leaves that may be found on any tree. There were instances, as in the case of prophet Balaam, where God allowed the gift to stay, even though the person's character did not reflect his connection or discipleship with God.

In fact, the prophet's life reflected a life that was not in sync with his discipleship.

2. A Christian leader is affected and transformed by God's grace and His Spirit. He or she is a person whose authority "is not won by promotion, but by many prayers and tears," as somebody said.

It is attained by confessions of sin, and much heart-searching and humbling before God; by self-surrender, a courageous sacrifice of every idol, a bold, deathless, uncompromising and uncomplaining embracing of the cross, and by eternal, unfaltering looking unto Jesus crucified," Samuel Logan Brengle.

3. A Christian leader is a person of God whose faith is being renewed and refined. He or she is a person who, touching the hand of God through faith, does not faint in life's crises and challenges.

A Christian leader is a person who can pray until something happens or until he or she is changed, or both.

> We need to learn to align, or rather subject, our attitudes, inmost affections, thoughts and actions to divine ideals and expectations, especially in leadership.

4. A Christian leader is a person of God who is love-filled, fulfilled and fulfilling. He or she knows and accepts that God loves him or her deeply to the point of dying on the cross. He or she is able to draw on that well of love and fill those who hunger and thirst.

5. A Christian leader is a person of God who is internally secure and unthreatened and can hold on to life even though storms rage and wreak havoc on his or her visible securities.

6. A Christian leader is a person of God who has allowed his or her intellect to be transformed and cleansed from the impurities that defile the soul and pollute the heart. His or her mental gates are vigilantly shut to evil progressively.

7. A Christian leader is a person of God who is humble enough to be of service to God and His people. If ever you have looked for God's character laundry, purification of character, and the washing of one's impurities at its best and fastest before the pearly gates, ask Him to make you His leader for His heaven-bound people. The primary calling is to become a disciple first and throughout to qualify as an effective Christian leader.

Leadership and character development are inseparable partners

1. "Leadership is a combination of strategy and character. If you must be without one, be without the strategy," Norman Schwarzkopf advised.

2. Christian leadership, unlike any other, demands that we do serious work on our characters, lest character or lack thereof speak louder than our voices and our message. "Character gives credibility. As a leader, your life either verifies or nullifies your life's work," said Douglas J. Rumford.

3. Christian leadership thrives on influence and influence on character – the person the leader truly is, both in his or her private and public life, determines the effectiveness of his or her leadership.

4. While Christian leadership is a God-given opportunity to develop Christian character for the kingdom, at the same time one's leadership is enhanced and authenticated by one's character.

5. We need to learn to align, or rather subject, our attitudes, inmost affections, thoughts and actions to divine ideals and expectations, especially in leadership. Unfortunately, as Christian leaders, many times we don't reflect the divine pattern, but miserably emulate the infidel's leadership value system.

6. The fruit of the Spirit must be evident in all of us, but more so in those who lead others.

7. More and more, our Christian organisations, Christian business meetings, Christian business relations and interpersonal relationships need to give evidence to our Christianity, not tendencies that are not in line with the nature of Christianity. God uses these to expose our unrefined and unconverted characteristics, to reveal our need of His transformation.

Leaders must prioritise the kingdom of God

1. Leaders must prioritise the kingdom of God because they are first and foremost called to be its obedient subjects, and their leadership calling may just be a means to that end after all.

2. Making the kingdom second or third in importance will only harm our testimony, as people will be quick to perceive that it is not important to us.

3. We must spend time with God more than with any other person because our agenda is God's agenda and no other, hence Paul urges that we pray incessantly.

4. What will it profit a leader to call everybody into the kingdom and be himself or herself an outcast in the end, and never see the fruit of his or her labour?

5. A great deal of time must be spent on our knees, conversing with God, seeking to understand and hear Him afresh, before, during and after our long,

> "Earn your success based on service to others,
> not at the expense of others."
> ~H. Jackson Brown, Jr. ~

difficult leadership journey.

6. Kingdom principles must make such a big impression on the leader that the people mistake him or her for the King, because he or she is the King's disciple and ambassador.

7. A Christian leader must be completely and thoroughly the subject of the Kingdom of Grace that he or she is not just inseparable from and synonymous with the Kingdom, but that those who come across his or her path feel the influence of heaven and are drawn to the kingdom.

Leadership attitudes, team and subordinate relations reveal transformation (Quotes)

1. "Christian leadership focuses more on helping others than commanding them. It is a life given to service," Roger L. Smalling.

2. "Worldly leaders use power to get things done for themselves, but Godly leaders use power to serve those they are called to lead and care for," Douglas J. Rumford.

3. "Worldly leaders want to be served; Godly leaders want to serve," (ibid.)

4. "Serving others to help them reach their full potential and treating fellow ministers [leaders] as equals is more than the mere duties of an office. It is a way of life," Roger L. Smalling.

5. "Jesus forbids His disciples to appoint to offices people with authoritarian attitudes," (ibid.)

The world's leadership norm is being pushy, being bossy bullies, showing off power, and flaunting authority, demanding, and expecting deifying service from subordinates and colleagues, reminding everyone of the power the leader possesses.

Jesus, observing this and knowing the human tendencies, appealed that it should not be so among His people and His leaders.

6. "Jesus revolutionises our understanding of leadership by teaching 'downward mobility.' In a most striking picture of servanthood, Jesus humbles Himself through obedience. By performing the task of a slave, Jesus models how far you are to go in serving others." Douglas J. Rumford.

7. Christian leaders must not be servants only when they want to get something out of the people, they must always be the servants of the people. Christian leaders, through God's transforming grace, must be of humble heart, mind and spirit consciously and deliberately, from the depths of their beings.

They must continually choose the serving attitude against the acceptable and self-assertive norms of power dynamics in the world in which they live and interact.

The world's leadership norm is being pushy, being bossy bullies, showing off power, and flaunting authority, demanding, and expecting deifying service from subordinates and colleagues, reminding everyone of the power the leader possesses. Jesus, observing this and knowing the human tendencies, appealed that it should not be so among His people and His leaders.

Christian leaders do not serve people for political and benefits

1. We are not in the service of people to serve our own interests. If you think that you serve people so that you can prosper, then you are wide off the mark. We serve and empower people so that they get to where they need to be in God's agenda for their lives. Our work is to help people to realise their God-given potential and service.

2. People are not stepping stones to our political or commercial end. They are our daily business, the primary reason we are called to serve.

3. Our service to people should not be motivated by profit but by love, compassion and goodwill. When we provide any service primarily because of money, then we love money more than people. When we have progressed beyond our love for money, we will serve people for their own sake whether there is money involved or not.

4. People's needs are not our bargaining chips or electioneering ticket but our

core business in the Kingdom. Meeting people's needs is our pleasure and helps us to fulfill our God-given mandate to feed the hungry, clothe the naked, house the homeless, heal the broken, take care of the poor, and love the neglected.

5. We serve people as a service to God as He requires it of us. We serve because God has asked us to and whether we hear a word of gratitude or not, we do it in obedience to Him who called us.

6. We realise it will cost us something, but we consider it a small sacrifice compared to God's sacrifice.

"The true leader serves. Serves people. Serves their best interests, and in so doing will not always be popular, may not always impress. But because true leaders are motivated by loving concern rather than a desire for personal glory, they are willing to pay the price," Eugene B. Habecker.

7. We do not serve to be saved, but serve because we are saved. We are saved for service to humanity! Leadership is serving people.

"The leader is the servant. So leadership is not having your way. It's not self-aggrandisement. But oddly it is for service. It is for the sake of the led. It is proper altruism," Desmond Tutu.

Transformation is God's competence and our responsibility

1. Inherent in all of us is our inability to change our lives, yet it is our responsibility to allow that change to be effected by God in us through His Spirit.

2. We must not think we are capable of changing on our own. (Jer 13:23) "Can an African change the colour of his skin? Can a leopard get rid of its spots? So what are the odds on you doing good, you who are so long-practiced in evil?"

3. We must not think we can or try to change other people, lest we become abrasive, forceful and coercive. We must humbly remember that it is God who transforms in both our case and in other people's cases.

4. We must realise that Spirit-led self-management is crucial in Christian

leadership, as it enhances one's witness. To lead effectively in God's affairs, we must seek God's transformation.

5. God could even use your willingness to obey his leadership call to bring about transformation in your life through your leadership vocation.

6. People expect the leader, more than anyone else, to demonstrate evidence of transformation, and that's the only way it will eventually catch on with people.

7. Some are more advanced in the Christian experience in some areas, and worse and immature in others. We must be careful not to be judgemental, dismissive, curt and harsh because we have progressed in an area in which somebody else is still intensely struggling. Patience with a weaker Christian sibling is also evidence of real transformation.

Christian leaders must demonstrate high standards

1. Both religious and secular people expect leaders to embody the highest values, and their disappointment is written across their hearts when leaders fail.

2. Don't think that the leader's privileges and responsibilities are different from those of the ordinary person.

This type of thinking leads to people excusing the shortcomings of the ordinary person but feeling an indignation and hopelessness when a leader falls short of basic ideals and expectations.

3. This expectation places a tremendous strain on the leader. He or she is probably aware that the people have pegged their hopes on their leader and that his or her fall might cause their hearts to stumble, especially when the leader has reached higher levels of leadership and experience.

4. (Luke 12:48) "Great gifts mean great responsibilities; greater gifts, greater responsibilities!" The higher the level of leadership the higher the expectations and the greater the responsibility to live out the ideals.
A leader is expected to be an embodiment of the ideals that he or she seeks to

> "Defeat is not defeat, unless accepted as a reality in your mind."
> ~ Bruce Lee ~

transmit. If reconciliation was Mandela's project, we had to see in him the spirit of forgiveness pervading his persona, helping him to deal with resentment of 27 years imprisonment and many years of ill-treatment.

We are attracted to him by his greatness of spirit, reconciliatory attitude, morality and character greater than our own.

5. Do your best to live up to the ideals of your calling, praying that you may not fall or fail. Leaders need to guard their lives and conduct more than the people they lead, lest the extent of their influence leads others astray with the defeatist self-exhortation that people usually express – if it is this hard for our leaders to live aright, how much more difficult it is for me, an ordinary person!

6. While you do your best to avoid the mistakes that are common to all persons and even our fore-bears, when you fail, do not shut the door and write yourself off.

Learn from David's repentance, not from Judas' cowardice and suicide. Embrace God's grace with courage which is ever stretched towards His children.

7. Do not fall or fail. If you fail today, rise up and walk again and again. That too might inspire some struggling person never to give up. Heroes, seemingly, are those who rise against the odds.

They are not perfect but their tenacity is inspirational. It does not matter how many times they have fallen, they rise up and try again every time they fall or falter; they have the courage to say, "I am sorry, I will try again," and they do until they get it right.

REALITY #3 God Prepares

God prepares His leaders every step of the way

1. God prepares His leaders even before they are born - pre-birth preparation. (Gen 25:23) "GOD told her, 'Two nations are in your womb, two peoples butting heads while still in your body. One people will overpower the other, and the older will serve the younger.'"

2. God prepares His leaders in childhood. (Isa 49:1) "Listen, far-flung islands, pay attention, faraway people: GOD put me to work from the day I was born. The moment I entered the world he named me."

3. God prepares His leaders through the years of youth (Exo 17:9) "Moses ordered Joshua: 'Select some men for us and go out and fight Amalek. Tomorrow I will take my stand on top of the hill holding God's staff.'"

4. God prepares His leaders in adulthood. (Exo 3:1) "Moses was shepherding the flock of Jethro, his father-in-law, the priest of Midian. He led the flock to the west end of the wilderness and came to the mountain of God, Horeb."

5. God's preparation is not always clear to the one being prepared and may be known reflectively.

6. The Caller, relentless in the pursuit of His plans, seeks the trusting cooperation of the leader He is preparing.

7. The leader usually does not always appreciate the preparation of God until he reaps its benefits later on and sees God's hand in hindsight.

God uses various circumstances to prepare His leaders

1. God used an insignificant and neglected environment to prepare the Messiah. (Isa 53:2) "The Servant grew up before God; a scrawny seedling, a scrubby plant in a parched field. There was nothing attractive about Him, nothing to cause us to take a second look."

It was unimaginable that a Messiah could come out of Nazareth, of all places.

2. God used suffering as well. (Isa 53:3) "He was looked down on and passed over, a man who suffered, who knew pain first-hand. One look at him and people turned away. We looked down on Him, thought He was scum."

3. Moses grew up under foreign nurture to become the liberator of Israel from Egyptian bondage. (Heb 11:24) "By faith Moses, when grown, refused the privileges of the Egyptian royal house."

4. To prepare Moses as a liberator-shepherd of the new nation, God used a lowly occupation. (Exo 3:1) "Moses was shepherding the flock of Jethro, his father-in-law, the priest of Midian. He led the flock to the west end of the wilderness and came to the mountain of God, Horeb."

5. David was exposed to political leadership, which was to be his future role, through Saul's need of a musician to soothe the king's depression. (1Sa 16:21) "David came to Saul and stood before him. Saul liked him immediately and made him his right-hand man."

6. It took a while before David was crowned as Israel's king. God used time to mature David, although he was anointed before going to serve Saul as a musician and eventually as a king.

7. God may use various circumstances in your life to prepare you for the leadership contribution that you need to make, now or in the future.

God uses various instruments to prepare and sharpen his leaders

1. Adversity develops the leader's resolve, stamina, patience, character, priorities, perspective and hope. For their sake and the sake of those they will lead, leaders are born in difficulty, raised in trying circumstances and graduated in tribulation.

2. Rejection drives the leader to the arms of God, the tranquility of prayer, the release of forgiveness, freedom to embrace anew, renewal of the soul, and a fresh meaning of love.

3. Isolation and lonesomeness give the leader time with God, an opportunity for vision clarification, re-evaluation, re-visioning, strategic thinking, rejuvenation and regrouping.

4. Brokenness and weakness teach reliance on God's grace, strength, love, forgiveness, healing, help, and results in humility.

5. Betrayal reminds the leader of God's unwavering love and friendship, places him or her in solidarity with Christ and magnifies God's steadiness, reliability, trustworthiness and assurance.

6. Crises and trials confirm the leader's need to depend on God, trusting Him to carry him or her through, be with the leader, carry the leader when it's too much, fully provide a way of escape, believing He will not allow the leader to be tested beyond his or her ability to endure, and assures the leader of God's sustenance.

7. Failures, challenges and setbacks are God's refreshment stations, His call to newness, to a fresh start, to refocus, to reveal new strategies and a release from the bondage of complacency.

Leadership preparation is a development process

1. God develops and matures His leaders over time. Time is God's classroom for His leaders. About 400 years went by with no sign of Joseph's dying prediction, or God's promise to Abraham.

The remnant of Jacob's family grew into a nation and their growth and prosperity evoked jealousy and nationalism in Egypt. Even in the oppression that sought to subject and reduce them to mere slaves, they grew into a great nation and the 'Pharoah who did not know Joseph' instituted measures to control their numbers.

God could have pulled them off the oven of oppression immediately when they were being ill-treated by the Egyptians. Instead God developed their national and religious identity under difficult conditions as they were to lead not just their contemporaries but their prosperity and future generations.

2. God takes all the time He needs to cover various aspects of the leader's development. Moses, who could have been perceived as matured for leadership, still needed to learn more lessons in the desert before taking up leadership. While in the desert classroom, he learns patience, humility and shepherd-like love for God's people.

3. God confines His timing to the leader's pace, readiness and maturity. Some leaders take 27 while others take 40 years to be fully developed, according to the extent of their influence that God envisages for them. The longer the development, it seems to me, the greater and long lasting the leader's contribution and legacy becomes.

4. We must pray for discernment of God's moves in our lives so that we do not delay or derail His development plans. Sometimes, in our haste, we miss the most important moves of God in our lives and delay his intended impact, or we lose heart and derail His plans for us.

5. Some leaders mature faster than others. A leader who is responsive to God's training is going to be ready earlier than others. We cannot expect the same or similar levels of maturity and delivery as we will be as fast or as slow we respond to God's actions in our lives.

It is the Holy Spirit that works on each leader and each leader must respond as openly to His work, otherwise we could be on parallel paths and yet come to our peak performance at different times.

6. Some leaders want to run ahead of God. Running ahead of God's plan, as seen in many instances, lead to aborted missions. I pray that we may know the distinction between bad and good timing and be able to choose the right time.

7. God develops leaders as He needs them and is least concerned about succession debates, succession moves or succession campaigns.

God is not in a hurry but moves at the right time. Jesus comes to our planet, at the fullness of time, according to Scripture. At the fullness of time, God's agenda will be realized and there is nothing anyone can do about an idea or leader whose time, mission and contribution have come.

Patiently submit to the divine discipline of delay

1. It may take a while before God's plan for your life is fulfilled, but it will come at the right time.

2. Good things come to those who wait profitably. God's leaders must avoid idle waiting. God's delays are an opportunity to work on the inner person.

3. God's timing is never behind or ahead of schedule; it's perfect.

4. Submitting to God's discipline gives God time to mature His leaders and to prepare the circumstances, and will save many a heartache and disappointment.

5. No one can resist an idea whose time has come, let alone a leader whose divinely ordained time has reached its fullness.

6. God's leaders must learn to patiently wait and murmur not, even if it seems as if it is taking forever for God's plan to be realised. Sarah's impatience led to devising a copout plan that seemed to work at first and kept the parties happy for a while, but led to frustration in the end.

7. The flip side of the coin is also true. The best leaders are not those that promote themselves as ready candidates for leadership. In fact, good leaders never feel ready or adequate to take leadership. And that is God's best time to make them best leaders, as they humbly rely on Him to make up for their inadequacies.

Take smaller responsibilities as God's preparation for greater things

1. Moses' and David's shepherding experiences were leading to national and international political leadership.

2. Samuel's leadership progressed from small temple chores to national spiritual responsibilities.

3. It was after Joshua served as a spy and as Moses' helper and General, that he was fit to become Israel's national political leader who led Israel's final

international expedition and settlement.

4. Peter and the other disciples who fished before they accepted Jesus' call did not realise that the enterprise of catching fish was the preparation for being fishers of people for Christ's kingdom.

5. The most unlikely and unpleasant responsibilities that a leader may have to do may turn out to be the best divinely ordained training for the leadership contribution you will be making sooner or later.

6. Whatever your assignment is now, do it as though it were your ultimate. Avoid spending too much of your time and energy on where you want to be rather than where you are. Excel right where you are and everything else shall be added to you.

7. Whenever you think you have arrived, look back and see how the Lord has been preparing you, and know that He still has other territories for you to conquer. Your greatest attainment today may be a molehill as you, in the hand of God, reach new heights every day.

God's preparation may be long, winding and apparently aimless as you impatiently wait

1. While still a lad, Joseph was told about his future leadership contribution through a dream.

2. When he revealed it to his family they not only ridiculed him for it, they made his life miserable. They could not accept that he, young as he was, was destined for greatness. This would not only exceed their imagined future for him, but surpass their own perceived greatness by far.

3. Thinking they were getting rid of him, Joseph's brothers sold him to foreigners as a cheap slave.

4. On arrival in Egypt where he was sold the second time, Joseph's leadership potential was quickly identified and he was placed in Potiphar's house as a chief attendant. This experience and exposure prepared him for the leadership role he was destined to fulfill later.

> The most unlikely and unpleasant responsibilities that a leader may have to do may turn out to be the best divinely ordained training for the leadership contribution you will be making sooner or later.

5. Potiphar's wife couldn't get her way with Joseph sexually and to save face she falsely accused him of sexual impropriety, for which he was immediately sent to prison.

By human reckoning this is a derailment or thwarting of God's plan for him, when in actual fact it paved the way for his prisoner-to-presidency career. Joseph's fellow inmates, whom he helped through his special gift of dream interpreting, forgot him after their release.

6. Joseph was eventually remembered and brought in to avert a looming national and international food crisis. He was appointed as the second-highest ranking official of the country and he saved the world from hunger because of his proposal, which was implemented as the national economic policy that keeps Egypt on the map for a long while, even in the seven years of international economic recession.

7. Eventually, in his senior years, Joseph has a déjà vu moment when his family literally bows down before him. Instead of the usual and much expected "I told you so" prefaced statement, he had allowed God to mature him, and so he said: (Gen 45:5) "But don't feel badly, don't blame yourselves for selling me. God was behind it. God sent me here ahead of you to save lives."

REALITY #4 God Empowers

God empowers the called through the Holy Spirit

1. (Gen 41:38) "Then Pharaoh said to his officials, 'Isn't this the man we need? Are we going to find anyone else who has God's spirit in him like this?'"

The Spirit of God fills and empowers those that are ready and willing, to the extent that those who observe, even though they may be believers of another faith different from yours, they will see empowerment by Him. Spirituality is developed in the lab of time and exposure to God's Spirit.

2. (Exo 31:1-5) "God spoke to Moses: 'See what I've done; I've personally chosen Bezalel son of Uri, son of Hur of the tribe of Judah. I've filled him with the Spirit of God, giving him skill and know-how and expertise in every kind of craft to create designs and work in gold, silver, and bronze; to cut and set gemstones; to carve wood—he's an all-around craftsman.'"

The Sprit of God not only fills and transforms our lives but gives us gifts, skills and abilities to do His work. Although you may have acquired your skills through training, the Spirit gives it more power and effect. He is the one who gives us all gifts, including what appears to be natural, spiritual or acquired through education. The Holy Spirit directs us to where He pleases and sees fit, and empowers us for the leadership contribution we are to make.

3. (Num 27:18) "GOD said to Moses, 'Take Joshua the son of Nun – the Spirit is in him! – and place your hand on him.'" God's Spirit as in the case of Joshua, dwells in willing leaders' hearts and gives them the necessary leadership attributes such as vision, courage and fortitude for the work they must do.

4. (1 Sam 16:13) "Samuel took his flask of oil and anointed him, with his brothers standing around watching. The Spirit of GOD entered David like a rush of wind, God vitally empowering him for the rest of his life. Samuel left and went home to Ramah."

David's life, with all its faults, was empowered by God's Spirit for the rest of his life from that point on. Unlike his predecessor, Saul, David was ever willing to change upon realising his errors and the Spirit of God empowered him out of his weakness.

Great leaders maintain a lifelong open relationship with God's Spirit, even when they err. God empowers them from that point forward, labours with them even in their moments of weakness, as long as they are willing to follow the Spirit's leading.

5. (Luke 4:18) "God's Spirit is on me; he's chosen me to preach the Message of good news to the poor, sent me to announce pardon to prisoners and recovery of sight to the blind, to set the burdened and battered free…"

God's Spirit empowers us to serve others. He wants to bring about a change in people's life. A Spirit empowered leader makes a difference in people's lives, his or her presence is a blessing to the disadvantaged and the struggling. A great and Spirit empowered leader inspires people out of their bondage, blindness, poverty, despair, fatigue, errors and apathy.

6. (Acts 1:8) "What you'll get is the Holy Spirit. And when the Holy Spirit comes on you, you will be able to be my witnesses in Jerusalem, all over Judea and Samaria, even to the ends of the world."

Spirit empowered leaders do progressive work, starting from the familiar and immediate to the unknown and un-entered. They are ever willing to expand, improve, and better their yesterday's achievements. They are not content with mediocre accomplishments. Success for Spirit empowered leaders is not historical but in the future, into the unknown and unrealised realities they bravely venture. The sky is not the limit!

7. (Acts 2:17) "'In the Last Days,' God says, 'I will pour out my Spirit on every kind of people: Your sons will prophesy, also your daughters; your young men will see visions, your old men dream dreams.'"

The same Spirit that empowered our forebears is among us, empowering all people irrespective of their age or gender, giving visions and dreams for the future. He is empowering our youth and our seniors for God's work. He empowers various people to greater heights than those achieved in the past.

Hear him whisper to Obama the message of hope in hopeless times, see him sustain Mandela with resilience in all adversity, hear him wrestle with the international community to return to God as Christian leaders proclaim Jesus' second coming.

God authorises the called and we will know them by their fruit

1. (2Ch 19:9) "He charged them: 'Do your work in the fear of GOD; be dependable and honest in your duties.'"

2. (Exo 23:21) "Pay close attention to him. Obey him. Don't go against him. He won't put up with your rebellions because he's acting on my authority."

3. (Heb 7:26) "So now we have a high priest who perfectly fits our needs: completely holy, uncompromised by sin, with authority extending as high as God's presence in heaven itself."

4. (Gal 1:1) "I, Paul, and my companions in faith here, send greetings to the Galatian churches. My authority for writing to you does not come from any popular vote of the people, nor does it come through the appointment of some human higher-up. It comes directly from Jesus the Messiah and God the Father, who raised him from the dead. I'm God-commissioned."

5. (Luke 22:29) "Now I confer on you the royal authority my Father conferred on me."

6. (Luke 10:20) "All the same, the great triumph is not in your authority over evil, but in God's authority over you and presence with you. Not what you do for God but what God does for you--that's the agenda for rejoicing."

7. (Mat 7:15) "Be wary of false preachers [leaders] who smile a lot, dripping with practiced sincerity. Chances are they are out to rip you off some way or other. Don't be impressed with charisma; look for character. (Mat 7:16) Who preachers [leaders] are, is the main thing, not what they say. A genuine leader will never exploit your emotions or your pocketbook. These diseased trees with their bad apples are going to be chopped down and burned (parenthesis is mine).

God enables those He calls to leadership

1. Whenever God calls a person to a task, He enables the called for the task at hand. He does not call a person to leadership without the necessary enablement and proper preparation.

2. Your experiences, unpleasant as they may sometimes be, may be allowed to happen to enable you to contribute to your leadership vocation effectively.

3. God has endowed every person with the competencies, natural abilities, capabilities, skills, spiritual gifts, gift mix and passion necessary for his or her leadership vocation.

4. (1Cor 12:7) "Each person is given something to do that shows him or her who God is. Everyone gets in on it, everyone benefits. All kinds of things are handed out by the Spirit, and to all kinds of people!"

5. Each person must identify his or her vocation and abilities that God has placed in his or her hands, even if he or she has to discover them through trial and error. This will enable him or her to make the contribution that he or she needs to make in God's business, and for the benefit of humanity.

6. Many would-have-been-great leaders lie two metres underground with untapped talent. Others, towards the end of their lives, regret that they have not left a legacy in the world by which current and future generations will fondly remember them.

While they lived they never thought to check what was providentially placed in their hands and hearts that would have made the world a special and a better place had they followed their calling.

What are we doing with our leadership advantages, opportunities, specialties, enabling (authority), endowments, contributions and passions that God has placed in our hands and hearts?

7. Some, realising what was placed in their hands and hearts, have sought to hide because they were afraid to brave the norm or venture into the unknown. We must all learn to bravely follow the voice that calls through enablement.

God empowers the called through training

1. Though Moses was brought up as an Egyptian prince for the first 40 years of his life, his first training was received from his mother, whose hopes in spite of slavery woes, served to introduce Moses to the true God.

2. While according to Egyptian standards, Moses was thought to be well educated, he still needed the training of God through the "University of the Desert" to learn to gently lead the people of God out of bondage.

3. Seeing an Israelite beaten by an Egyptian slave driver, Moses probably thought it was time to intervene, or he simply lost his patience and possibly thought it was time to begin the process of liberating his people. God needed to train him to be patient and He brought Moses out of Egyptian comfort and allowed him to go through the desert experience that effectively and patiently prepared him for what was to come.

4. Only when God had trained him for another 40 years in Arabic Midian was he called to fulfill his childhood dream of liberating the Israelites from Egyptian bondage. Only when Moses had himself become a slave and shepherd of Jethro, when he had communed with God and nature, was he ready for a commission to be the new nation's deliverer.

5. We appreciate the value of Moses' training of 80 years, especially in his last 40 years. Moses' Egyptian education and training, which was sponsored by God, was employed in his leadership as the liberator, General and leader of Israel. His years of communion with God in the desert prepared him for his leadership role as the prophet and pastor par excellence. His training made him Israel's best meek leader, a rather disinterested iconic leader. For Mandela it took 27 years in prison to make a remarkable leadership contribution that would last a lifetime and beyond.

6. God uses various means to empower His leaders and to train them to be equal to the specific contribution that He intends they should make on behalf of His people.

7. God's training does not dilute the leader's calling; it rather enhances and sharpens it.

> "If I am young and wrong, then you are right [to look down on my youthful ignorance.] But if I am young and right, what does my age matter?"
> ~ Antigone Aesculus ~

God develops and matures the capacities of the called

1. Joshua and many leaders started with what appeared to be mundane tasks, but were being trained for greater responsibilities.

2. Today's limitations may be tomorrow's capabilities as God challenges, stretches, harnesses, improves, builds, strengthens and fosters the leader's potential.

3. Leaders respond differently to God's promptings and will be ready at different times, regardless of age and experience. Experience is helpful in making a wiser contribution but not essential to start making a contribution.

4. While the number of years of experience assumes quality and maturity, this does not apply in every person's case. We have leaders whose maturity, achievements and contribution, quantitatively and qualitatively, far outweigh their years.

On the other hand, we have leaders, who though they have lived longer, have little to show for their many years. The leader's pace of maturity depends on a number of factors such as the person's ability to respond to the Spirit of God's preparation on his or her life. We must therefore careful to measure person's maturity according to age.

5. Josiah began his political leadership at the age of eight and ruled for 31 years. His leadership was marked with remarkable religious reform that not only removed gods and places of idolatry, but removed the gods and the places

"Guard your light and protect it.
Move it forward into the world and be fully
confident that if we connect light
to light to light, and join the lights together
of the one billion young people in our
world today, we will be enough
to set our whole planet aglow."
~ Hafsat Abiola ~

erected for idol worship by his predecessors such as Kings Ahaz, Hezekiah, Solomon, Manasseh and so on. It was during this youthful king's leadership that a copy of the law was recovered and read publicly, the Covenant with God was renewed and the Temple of worship was restored.

6. Of the young Josiah's outstanding leadership contribution, it is written: (2Ki 23:25) "There was no king to compare with Josiah, neither before nor after, a king who turned in total and repentant obedience to God, heart and mind and strength, following the instructions revealed to and written by Moses. The world would never again see a king like Josiah."

7. The outstanding qualities of Josiah or the trustworthiness of the servant in Mat 25:21 could become true of any person today, irrespective of experience, gender, background or age. "The master says to His servant: 'Well done, good and trustworthy servant! Since you have been trustworthy with a small amount, I will put you in charge of a large amount. Come and share your master's joy.'"

God gives power and all power must serve His purposes

1. God, in the first place, as Dan 2:21 says . . . "changes the seasons and guides history, He raises up kings and also brings them down, He provides both intelligence and discernment . . . "

2. God gives power to leaders for their work and decides the length and extent of their power. He keeps all leaders in check through accountability to Him and to the people that work with the leaders.

3. When God gives power, He gives it for the advancement of His people, not for abuse by the leader. When leaders abuse power, they are not acting in line with the Giver of power but outside His mandate.

4. God gives us power to test our character, which is revealed in our use of it. Abraham Lincoln concedes. "Nearly all men can stand adversity, but if you want to test a man's character, give him power."

5. Leaders, especially Christian leaders, in whatever leadership context, must control their use or interaction with their God-given power. They must be absolutely sure that they are not using their power to their own advantage and to the disadvantage of the people that they are leading. We must control our

human nature, which is always seeking to assert itself through power and its display. "Power is when you have every justification to kill someone, and then you don't," Oscar Shindler.

6. A leader and the people he or she leads are safe when he or she wields power in fear of, in tune with, as emulation of and to the glory of God, who is all powerful yet circumspectly and patiently persuades His creatures with utmost love and respect without a show of or resort to His majestic power.

7. Each of us, when Jesus returns, will give an account to God on how we have used our privileges and opportunities in our lifetime on earth, (Rom 14:12).

There are various kinds of power but not all power is suitable for God's leaders

1. Leaders wield various forms of power, some of which are unpleasant and must be avoided, especially by Christian leaders. All leaders are given some degree of inherent or natural power, which comes by virtue of their leadership vocation, or sometimes the positions they hold.

The danger is when leaders do not realise that they have this kind of power and seek to regularly remind the people they lead, which is an indication that the reminding leader is uncertain of his or her power and is insecure in his or her position. Margaret Thatcher is instructive when she says: "Being powerful is like being a lady. If you have to tell people you are, you aren't."

2. Leaders also have ascribed power that their followers usually associate with the personality of the leader, who may or may not occupy any officially elected leadership position. This kind of leadership power comes as a result of perceived abilities, or the confidence that people have in the leader as a person.

The danger with this leadership power is that some leaders can be lax and careless and can be allowed to get away with little or no criticism, while others in the same situation will not be given that liberty. The perceived abilities are not always real. The leader who has ascribed power is not always aware of such respect and credit.

"The primary threat to nature and people today comes from centralising and monopolising power and control.

Not until diversity is made the logic of production will there be a chance for sustainability, justice and peace.

Cultivating and conserving diversity is no luxury in our times:
it is a survival imperative."
~ Vandana Shiva ~

> A leader and the people he or she leads are safe when he or she wields power in fear of, in tune with, as emulation of and to the glory of God, who is all powerful yet circumspectly and patiently persuades His creatures with utmost love and respect without a show of or resort to His majestic power.

3. Assumed power happens when a leader overtly or subtly, gradually or rapidly assumes more power than he or she should exercise. The people with whom he or she works allow this to happen. Lack of accountability, transparency and abuse of power abound in such cases as the leader's control increases and goes unrestrained.

4. Competence power is also attributed to the leader because of the leader's knowledge, expertise, skills, wisdom, experience and specialty, or a combination of all of these.

5. The most dangerous form of power for Christian leaders is induced or manipulative power. This type of power is usually attributed to a leader because of some sensed or real trepidation or fear that people feel, because the leader is thought, rumoured or known to be capable of forcing his or her way on subordinates by giving them pleasant or painful rewards such as promotion, demotion or ostracism.

6. Relational power usually occurs in a situation where leaders are able to relate to the people in a free environment in which the people feel an attraction and loyalty to their leader and his or her ideals. The leader influences the people to cooperate through genuine love, interest and care in a context of non-coercive interactive persuasion.

7. Serving power would be harnessing and harmonising all the positive forms of power such as relational power, competence power and inherent power, as

well as ascribed power to serve the people and meet their needs. "Power at its best is love implementing the demands of justice. Justice at its best is love correcting everything that stands against love," Martin Luther King, Jr.

There's probably no better caution that one could receive than Nelson Mandela's counsel to his successor Thabo Mbeki as ANC president in 1997: "One of the temptations of a leader who has been elected unopposed is that he may use his powerful position to settle scores with his detractors, marginalise them, and in certain cases, get rid of them and surround himself with yes-men and-women. A leader must keep the forces together, but you can't do that unless you allow dissent… people should even be able to criticize the leader without fear or favour," (as quoted by Mark Gevisser in Thabo Mbeki: The Dream Deferred.)

REALITY #5 God Sharpens

Crises call for leadership and courage

1. A moment of crisis may be God's way of awakening and sharpening a leader's inert or sensed vocation that he or she may not have previously realised.

2. A genocide was threatening to obliterate the Jewish nation that remained in Persia after the great national homecoming. Mordecai, son of Jair, who served as a senior civil servant in the Persian metropolis called Susa, discovered the plot and tried to enlist Esther's intervention.

3. When Esther, who was a queen at the time, heard it through her attendants, she did not want to be involved at all as her life as a queen and a human being would be abruptly ended. Little did she realise that this was God's opportunity meant for her to really shine as the star her name claimed she was.

It was her call to make that single courageous leadership contribution that would make her one of the entries in the Middle East Guinness Book of Records for herself, her people and more so for her God. Mordecai, her mentor and uncle, persuasively encouraged her to shine for Christ.

4. She had allowed her fear of a perceived sense of inadequacy, a feeling of irrelevance, detachment from the great crisis, a lack of faith, vision and empathy to direct her initial reaction. After the Mordecai perspective made its way into her heart, and her face-to-face encounter with destiny, she knew with clarity what she needed to do.

5. Once her vision was sharpened, her realisation of the gravity of the situation awoke in her a sense of urgency and she acted decisively. Today we, as in previous generations, hold her up to our children to be admired as an epitome of unselfish courage who possessed selfless leadership.

6. Realising she was the person for the moment or the hour, that she was made a leader for that crisis, she uttered the profound words that should be every Christian leader's motto as exemplified in the cross: (Esther 4:16) "If I die, I die."

7. "The greatest want of the world is the want of men [and women] who will not be bought or sold, men who in their inmost souls are true and honest, men who do not fear to call sin by its right name, men whose conscience is as true to duty as the needle to the pole, men who will stand for the right though the heavens fall," Ellen G White.

Sometimes God sharpens his leaders through adversity

1. Adversity breaks no bones but strengthens the leader's spirit and resolve. Great leaders are those who have learnt to confront their unfavourable circumstances and fears head on, reversing their vacillation with faith, courage, hope and resilience.

2. Resilience is evoked, displayed, tested and improved in adversity. To begin is easy. Almost anyone can begin the spiritual and leadership journey, but to take it to the finish, leaders need staying power and resilience.

3. Character is the essence of the person, the stuff beneath the veneer and the façade. Character remains when we are stripped bare of everything else in this life. Great leaders' characters are revealed and baked in the oven of adversity.

4. Adversity helps the leader to clarify priorities. We often forget what matters most and sometimes through adversity we are reminded of what is most important.

5. Adversity brings or refreshes the leader's perspective, which may have been lost in the course of life. After life's rough patches, a person's capacity for the appreciation of something as simple as raindrops is increased.

6. To learn to keep hope and courage alive even in the ugly face of adversity is to be halfway through God's plan for a fulfilled life of faith. To smile and praise God through the storms of life means you have arrived and have gained new heights in your Christian leadership experience.

7. Through all unfavourable circumstances we must always be hopeful, trusting that things will be better tomorrow, clutching God's hand unwaveringly till the storm passes over.

"One isn't necessarily born with courage, but
one is born with potential.
Without courage, we cannot practice
any other virtue with consistency.
We can't be kind, true, merciful,
generous or honest."
~ Maya Angelou ~

The ultimate purpose that God allows adversity to come our way is not to break us, but to reveal inherent weaknesses that would not otherwise have been discovered, and it's a divine invitation to transformation and new strength.

Imagine the end and keep focused on it

1. Leadership requires that we see beyond the ordinary; that we believe in great possibilities, that we grasp the Invisible, that we keep the end in mind despite present realities, that we keep hope alive.

2. No doubt, giants are real. They are born in life in the form of stumbling blocks, troubles and fears that may come up almost everywhere in the leadership path. Even though giants are real, the reality is that most giants are grown to great proportions in our imaginations.

We tend to magnify a small hurdle beyond our ability or God's ability to handle. Though they appear great, God is greater than the greatest real or imagined giants or our fears of giants. Great leaders, like Joshua and Caleb, see giants for what they are, grasshoppers in the eyes of God.

3. Great leaders refuse to see themselves as grasshoppers because they have imaginative faith larger than any obstacle. They allow God to sharpen their vision of the realities they seek to create or realise.

While others see giants growing in front of them or in their heads, God's leaders see God majestically seated on His throne, an assurance that He is in control and undisturbed.

4. Isaiah and Stephen could disregard the momentary torture because their eyes had caught a vision of their bodies restored in eternity, counting it joy to suffer for the cause.

5. Your hour of adversity is not eternal, though it feels that way. Others before you have survived to tell the story. Your tribulations will pass soon, and later on they will be moments in history as you recall them in eternity.

6. John could endure the torture and pain because his eye had caught a vision of reality beyond the present orb.

7. Whatever your circumstances, your hurdles, stumbling blocks, your giants or your mountains, let your imaginative faith grasp your God enthroned, the God who is greater than all your giants, and who will eventually realise His purposes eventually for you and for the universe.

Our vision and focus may need to be crystallised

1. Sometimes our vision of what needs to be done or what we are called to do is not so clear. We spend a lot of our energy and resources doing everything, and accomplishing nothing in the end.

2. God takes the time to sharpen our blunted and blurred vision of His intended reality and our skewed focus on it.

3. God, in His grace, sharpens our vision and focus to give us a clear sense of purpose and mission. We learn to do that which matters most for God, His people and ourselves.

4. It seems that Daniel is best suited to become a prophet of God after he has been displaced and thrust into unfamiliar territory. It takes a number of years for him to realise his special leadership contribution, from Nebuchadnezzar's nightmarish dream until Belshazzar's mysterious writing on the wall.

His vision crystallises with time as he is shown what was to be partially fulfilled in his time and fully realised in the last days.

We not only see the principle of recapitulation in the prophecies we distinctly remember him for, but we also see it in his life as each experience progresses towards a fuller picture and maturity.

In the end he probably dies a fulfilled person, not only because he has been faithful as a civil servant for King Nebuchadnezzar and as a prophet of God, but also because he catches the vision of Israel's restoration in the earthly and heavenly Jerusalem.

5. Moses took longer to have his vision and focus crystallised, although the liberation of his people was his childhood dream that his mother cleverly instilled in him. It was in the desert of Midian that he would have leaped for joy as God offered him an opportunity to not only see his dream realised, but also to be the catalyst in its fulfillment.

> "Cautious, careful people, always casting about to preserve their reputation and social standing,
> never can bring about a reform.
> Those who are really in earnest must be willing to be anything or nothing in the world's estimation, and publicly and privately, in season and out,
> avow their sympathy with despised and persecuted ideas and their advocates, and bear the consequences."
> Susan B. Anthony

6. Perhaps South Africa would not have realised a peaceful transition from apartheid to the democratic dispensation if it had not been for Nelson Mandela's 27 years of imprisonment. This experience not only matured this stalwart, but gave him iconic status and impact from a small village to the global village. His articulation of a non-racial and united society had to be personally practised in prison, to mature him to effectively handle the would-have-been volatile transition in post-apartheid South Africa.

Mandela's legacy, among other things, is adorned with the beautiful exemplification of the Christian principle of unpretending forgiveness, genuine love for one's former persecutors and a vision of transforming love that has touched our world's hearts forever. Maybe it is the scarcity of such examples that makes the world fail to see the divine alternative to war, strife, revenge and conquest.

7. It may take a long while before we see as clearly as God wants us to see. God may need to sharpen our blurred vision and focus before He realises the purpose for which He calls us.

God aligns his leaders' impulses with the divine ideals

1. It is easy to miss it in the forest, yet it's clear; for God's leaders to have an impact in the world, they should align their lives, impulses, and values to Divine ideals. The leaders' thoughts, language and practice must reflect God's way.

2. God is love. He is the essence of love and every good that goes with love. Everything that God does in both His historic and personal interaction with humanity is driven, guided, controlled and filtered through love. The cross is the pinnacle of His gracious love, which sums up all history, prophecy and future in love.

3. The leaders of God should fall on, err on the side of, fall and break on, rise and stand on, be aligned with and be known for nothing else but love and all its shades, after the divine similitude.

4. (Mat 22:37) "And He said to him; 'You shall love the Lord your God with all your heart and with all your soul and with all your mind.' (Mat 22:38) This is the great and first commandment. (Mat 22:39) And a second is like it; 'You shall love your neighbour as yourself.' (Mat 22:40) On these two commandments depend all the Law and the Prophets." (quoted from the English Standard Version)

5. (1Cor 13:13) "But for right now, until that completeness, we have three things to do to lead us toward that consummation: Trust steadily in God, hope unswervingly, love extravagantly. And the best of the three is love."

6. Maybe Martin Luther King Jr. had a glimpse of this reality when he said; "He who is devoid of the power to forgive is devoid of the power to love." H. Jackson Brown echoed a similar sentiment in his statement; "Never forget the three powerful resources you always have available to you: love, power and forgiveness." "Without forgiveness, there's no future," said Desmond Tutu.

7. (1Cor 13:3) "If I give everything I own to the poor and even go to the stake to be burned as a martyr but I don't love, I've gotten nowhere. So, no matter what I say, what I believe, and what I do, I'm bankrupt without love."

CALLED TO LEAD

> (Those who lead give sight to
> those who follow.
> Those who follow give life to
> those who lead)
> ~ Pauline Tangiora ~

God sharpens your experience

1. Many leaders are content with yesterday's experiences, recounting them for years to come as though God's experience taps have run dry. When we have stopped singing a new song it is because we have not allowed the Virtuoso to play us anew.

2. It is not God who has run out of ideas for new and fresh stories of grace in our lives; it is we who choose to shut ourselves to new experiences with God.

3. We must allow God to quicken us from our lethargy and give us new spiritual and leadership experiences, or we will perish in the Valley of Dry Bones.

4. In the Valley Of Dry Bones, where many are citizens, the stench of death and the rattle of lifeless bones have the potential to bring down those who are still breathing and walking. Stay away from the citizens of the Valley of Dry Bones. They will crush your spirit and your desire to live. They seek company in their country to make them feel good about their citizenship.

5. But you do not belong there. You belong to the green pastures, lush with hope, and ever-fresh experiences and energy.

6. Drink from the well that never runs dry, which is filled up every morning.

7. Fill your cup with positives, trusting the Great Mathematician who adds by subtracting, and multiplies by dividing.

"The person who tries to live alone will not
succeed as a human being.
His heart withers if it does not answer
another heart.
His mind shrinks away if he hears only
the echoes of his own thoughts
and finds no other inspiration."
~ Pearl S. Buck ~

"The interdependency of humankind,
the relevance of relationship,
the sacredness of creation is ancient,
ancient wisdom."
~ Rebecca Adamson ~

As iron sharpens iron

1. Ubuntu or humanness in creation and in culture demands that we connect with one another in interdependence.

2. A person is a person because others have touched him or her in human connectedness and relatedness. This umbilical cord remains as long as we live, and it becomes our God-given channel of mutual beneficiation through which we can grow and renew our lives from the interaction.

3. As no person lives as an island, no leader thrives in solitary dissociations. While it is true that some can 'successfully' insulate themselves from social interaction for whatever reason, we live much better with one another.

4. It is alleged that to be in leadership is to be ostracised. It is by self-imposed and self-restrained choices that a leader lives in islands of aloofness, of distant connections with both fellow leaders and those he or she seeks to reach. How would one grow and how would one provide meaningful leadership if he or she is not connected with people?

5. God has graciously provided friends, colleagues, even those we lead for the renewal and sharpening of wise leaders.

6. These relationships provide many opportunities for growth in intellectual, spiritual and relational areas of human existence and leadership vocation.

7. In African social thinking, the saying Umntu ngumntu ngabantu, means that no person is an island and that you are a person because of collective humanity.

In the same way as Reuel Khoza asserts in his epic book Let Africa Lead, "inkosi yinkosi ngabantu – a king is a king because of his subjects." Leadership, while divinely ordained, is necessitated, mandated and validated by people. No leader is a leader without people or those that are being led.

A leader needs the people in the same way the people need the leader, otherwise his or her leadership is irrelevant, loses meaning and growth potential. "The self cannot be self without other selves. Self concern without concern for others is like a tributary that has no outward flow to the ocean; stagnant, still and stale it lacks both life and freshness," (Khoza, 2006). "In society at large, while we may be aware of our mutual dependence and subscribe to notions of human fraternity, we often fail to act accordingly.

The server leader [revision of Servant Leader] is the chief agent of striving towards harmony in community. He or she reminds us of our human ties, constantly getting us to see that we are interdependent and need each other as family members need each other. People are people because of other people," ((ibid.))

Great leaders let God sharpen them through incarnate social interactions to be able to effectively serve humanity, a classical proverbial example being the Incarnation of Jesus, who became one of us to make us one with God.

REALITY #6 God Replaces

When your task is accomplished

1. Several people in Scripture were engaged in various construction and time-related projects of various kinds. Their leadership involvement or participation was as short-lived as the projects themselves.

2. Since it is God who calls, He determines when your task in the grand scheme of things is accomplished when He causes or allows circumstances to lead to your leadership contribution to be discontinued. For your peace of mind and sanity, take the hand of God because He works in mysterious ways. When one door shuts, another opens elsewhere. Keep alert to God's leading for new opportunities where a multitude of doors will open.

3. Daniel and Israel find themselves rudely uprooted from their familiar and comfortable zone to a foreign and hostile context. Their discomfort becomes God's window to speak to the whole world about things that will happen, finally resulting in King Nebuchadnezzar's conversion. Your misfortunes could be someone else's blessings.

4. When your task is done where you are, God will place you where you are needed most or where you will have more impact.

5. Often leaders resist God's replacement and/or relocation because they have become comfortable with their habitual scenery or contribution. Some leaders force their stay and attempt to defy their sell-by date, and in some instances, cause more damage than the good they have accomplished in their former years.

6. But God may be allowing your replacement to move you from the ordinary to the extra-ordinary and your resistance could be depriving you of that special experience that God thinks you need before He sends you on another errand.

7. Leaders must build into their psyche the flexibility and adaptability to be relocated, replaced, removed, re-channeled, reassigned, redeployed, or recalled.

After you have reached your peak

1. Christian leadership by its nature is a change-driven enterprise, seeking change in people's corporate and personal lives. You are in leadership to effect change.

2. You cannot be content with cosmetic change, for God is looking for wholesale change, even though it may be effected gradually or in parts.

3. As a leader guided by God's movements and principles, you must continually innovate. When you no longer innovate, you are likely to become irrelevant.

4. After you have reached your peak, when your attitude towards change is hostile, it's time to pass the baton to the next generation.

5. After you reach your peak, when you cease to see a need to innovate, your experience will be valuable as a mentor or consultant or adviser to someone else with more creative energy, who will carry the work forward, 1 Kings 2:1, 2.

6. We make specific and special contributions in God's work, but there comes a time when we reach our peak and we have nothing more to change or contribute. Then God replaces us.

7. While God replaces His leaders, He never forgets their contribution even though others may forget. He will remember the hard work put in for His sake and takes pride in His servants.

When you reach your expiry date

1. Human beings are not inexhaustible. We all have an expiry date though it's not known to any of us.

2. We are given an opportunity to play in the space of history, making whatever temporal contribution we need to make to improve other people's lives.

3. There are three phases to human life and leadership: picking up, peaking up and packing up. At the last stage we slow down and eventually pack up. We reach our sell-by date and stop making any contribution.

4. As we reach our peak, which is at the height of our life span and our leadership contribution, we must have identified and mentored young talent to carry the leadership cause forward.

5. God's cause must not suffer, it must carry on. When Moses packed up, fresh blood in the person of Joshua, whom Moses had mentored, was brought in to replace him. God calls Joshua to fill the gap and carry on from Moses' unfinished business. God says: (Josh 1:2) "Moses my servant is dead. Get going. Cross this Jordan River, you and all the people. Cross to the country I'm giving to the People of Israel."

6. Sometimes leaders reach their expiry date before death in terms of being able to make a contribution. This is when the health of God's servants collapses and God allows His servants to be replaced while they are still alive.

7. All things remaining equal, when God replaces a leader, it is no judgement on the incumbent. God's leaders are to learn to let go and let God.

When your leadership contribution is no longer relevant

1. Samuel is a prophet-priest-king in Israel and Israelites demand a king, as they would like to be like other nations, among other things. Under God's guidance, Saul is chosen as the first king of Israel.

The effect of this decision is a move from theocracy to democracy, and the separation of the religious and political functions. Samuel's role as the quasi-head of the state of Israel is curtailed to the ecclesiastical or religious functions, and his quasi-political leadership is no longer relevant.

2. The beginning of elective and hereditary monarchy in Israel unleashes a new expectation for the royal first-born males, resulting in a culture of competition for positions that in some instances lead to bloodshed. Saul's son, Jonathan, who serves as an army general, is expected to take the reins from his father.

Jonathan, a loyal friend of David, who may or may not have been aware that he was not chosen to replace his father Saul as king over Israel, seems very aware, supportive and protective of David as a person with a distinct leadership contribution and mission to live for.

He is happy to support David from the day David returns as a national champion up until his (Jonathan's) untimely death during the battle of Gilboa.

3. Great leaders are able to support other leaders as long as it is within their power to do so, and are willing to take a secondary place in instances where their leadership contribution is placed as secondary to others.

4. Great Christian leaders do not think of themselves as indispensable, or always necessary for God to realise His plans. They accept their historically confined opportunity and realise it as God's grace.

5. We are called up to lead for a time, for a specific purpose, and when our particular contribution is no longer relevant, we must be replaced.

6. Often we think it is the people that replace or reject our contribution, but it may just be God telling us to move on and to make a contribution elsewhere.

7. It is possible to talk of a leader who is no longer relevant for the particular people, or contribution. We may talk of a leader who has overstayed his or her time.

When you have failed to live up to the divine call

1. Saul was called to national political leadership but failed to live up to that call. Saul allowed his insecurities and disobedience to derail and eventually ruin his leadership vocation. His leadership, as it is with all of us, was to be in line with Divine direction but Saul failed to subject his leadership to Divine leadership.

2. Unfortunately he had to be told: (1Sa 15:26) "But Samuel refused: 'No, I can't come alongside you in this. You rejected God's command. Now God has rejected you as king over Israel.'"

3. When we have failed to live up to the call, the verdict is (1Sa 15:28) "as Samuel said: 'God has just now torn the kingdom from you, and handed it over to your neighbour, a better man than you are.'"

4. God is graciously going to work with each of us until we blatantly reject His instructions and lifestyle. When we reject the voice of God and our cup of iniquity is full, God, in His grace, replaces us with somebody else who will

be better than we are, in that he or she will be responsive to the promptings of God's Spirit.

5. Leaders will do well to always check if they are in line with the call, and always be ready to make adjustments where necessary, or they will be recalled and replaced.

6. When we are replaced because we have failed, we must humbly accept that we are not indispensable and must not make our replacement's life difficult in any way. Anything we can do to help the incoming leader, at their request, we must willingly do.

7. We cannot do as we please and just hope things will remain as usual. God's actions may be graciously delayed to allow us to repent, but if we refuse to listen, we must go sooner or later.

When the caller thinks you must rest

1. There are times when God in His wisdom, as in the instance of David, restricts the leader's contribution.

2. David was known as the beloved from his name and his personality, but more so because of his relationship with God.

He had demonstrated what a person and leader of God should be in the manner he treated Saul, who was hunting him because of jealousies, as well as in his treatment of Saul's grandson, Mephibosheth. Both were at his mercy and deserved to fall by David's sword. Instead of retaliating, David showed mercy to Saul and his posterity.

3. David, despite his track record of faltering, was very responsive to God's Spirit, and he turned out to be God's best monumental demonstration of grace. Not only did God forgive him for his sometimes atrocious sins, God honoured his beloved in many ways.

4. David so intensely wanted to build God's temple. He planned the temple project and gathered all materials needed for the construction. He was told that he was not to build the temple himself.

> When your time is up, allow the next leader to move in without your ego causing you to stumble in the way...

5. David had been a man of war and had also shed innocent blood. God thought his beloved friend should rest this time. Perhaps, God would not allow that the temple which was to be a pointer to the Innocent Victim would be built by a person who had shed innocent blood.

6. When he heard the news, he gladly accepted the verdict as all great leaders should.

7. Sometimes we may so want to do a special project or make a special contribution for God, but God may think otherwise for whatever reason.

It does not diminish our value to Him nor does it disregard our contribution. Just like David did, let's accept God's wisdom, even though we may not quite understand it.

When your replacement is ready

1. John the Baptist was a great leader who knew and accepted his leadership calling and mission. He was called to prepare the way for the Messiah.

2. John wielded so much influence through his powerful preaching that many people came to listen to him and to be baptised. His popularity reached such great heights that they confused him with Elijah and the Messiah.

3. But John knew he was not the Messiah. He knew that Jesus, his younger cousin, was the Messiah. John knew he was just the forerunner for the Messiah to pave the way for Jesus' leadership extraordinaire. John did not allow his opinion of self to cloud his function and relationship with Christ.

4. John did his assigned part without reservation or prejudice until Jesus was

ready to take centre stage. John, in the interim, predicted and acknowledged Jesus as the one who was greater than he and he felt unworthy to untie His shoe laces.

5. From Jesus' baptism, done by John against his wishes, John's leadership had completed its course and his life was terminated by execution six months after what appeared to be Jesus' inauguration.

6. John magnanimously did what he needed to do, but when his replacement was ready, he voted with his heart, voice and feet; (John 3:30) "This is the assigned moment for him to move into the centre, while I slip off to the sidelines."

7. What a lesson for all of us to learn! When our replacement is ready we must graciously slip off to the sidelines without resistance, resentment or regret. When your time is up, allow the next leader to move in, without your ego causing you to stumble in the way "because the cause is more important than personal popularity," John Maxwell.

REALITY #7 God Rewards

Great is your reward

1. The God who calls has promised to reward His people and leaders when He returns. When Christ comes again, He shall welcome all of us to his heavenly riches and reward each of us for the work we have done.

2. (1Cor 15:58) "With all this going for us, my dear, dear friends, stand your ground. And don't hold back. Throw yourselves into the work of the Master, confident that nothing you do for Him is a waste of time or effort."

3. Even before the heavenly reward, we from time to time experience a sense of fulfillment when the task is accomplished.

4. It's rewarding to see a change of a situation that was worse before you came in.

5. Probably the most rewarding is to see a person's life changed for the better because of your intervention in that person's life.

6. Often you do not realise its impact and importance, but your own life changes because of your leadership vocation or contribution and that in itself is a pre-heaven reward.

7. We must always remember, now and in the future, that even rewards are God's continued expression of redemptive grace, not because we deserve to be rewarded.

> Even before the heavenly reward, we from time to time experience a sense of fulfillment when the task is accomplished.

LEADERSHIP VALUES

"Values are the foundational truths that anchor our lives, the things that matter to us most, the non-negotiable characteristics that best define our identities ... When people take time and make the effort to focus on their values – the things that matter most to them – they are much better positioned to thrive in the face of life's daily pressures. Winning individuals, families and organizations have identified their values and apply them to daily living. When they face crucial decisions and times of crisis, value driven people are able to respond quickly and appropriately."
~ Gary Collins ~

VALUE #1 Honesty and Trustworthiness

1. Leaders need to build and maintain the trust of people they lead and to this end leaders must be honest; they must be in the habit of telling the truth consistently. They must be "men [and women] who in their inmost souls are true and honest," Ellen G White.

2. Leaders must also be honest enough to also want to hear the truth, even though the truth may hurt or displease them or undermine their false sense of security.

3. Ken Blanchard and Phil Hodges say, "Being vulnerable is one of the most powerful things you can do to build a team and to build relationships with people you're leading. They know that you're not perfect, so don't act as if you are. More often than not, they know your imperfections long before you reveal them," (Blanchard & Hodges, 2005).

4. As leaders, we must be careful not to surround ourselves with advisers and audiences that only flatter our egos and never correct our missteps.

5. (Prov 27:6) "The wounds from a lover are worth it; kisses from an enemy do you in." The writing may be on the wall and we may not see it because the ones who see it don't want to tell us, lest we be offended. At the same time it is also true that "All of us need someone, or several someones, who will love us enough to still be our friend no matter what they learn about us," (Blanchard & Hodges, 2005).

6. A leader who lets his or her judgment be crowded and clouded by the uncritical multitude will soon look for these cheerers and not find them anywhere, as they will have gone to flatter another one who may still be on his or her feet at the time.

7. When we have erred as leaders and our mistakes are pointed out, and it should not matter by whom, honesty demands that we admit without justifying or excusing our wrong. (Jam 5:16) "Make this your common practice: Confess your sins to each other and pray for each other so that you can live together whole and healed…"

A leader who is honest with him or herself, with people he or she leads, is open about his or her shortcomings and errors, and is able to apologise when wrong, is greatly respected.

A leader who acknowledges his blindness and need of grace will help his or her people to not only see him as a fellow struggler but a person who can be trusted to lead them to greater heights than they have so far found themselves in the morass of failure and struggling. But pretending yet struggling leaders are an offense to people's sensibilities, aspirations and hopes.

> "Ethics must begin at the top of an organization. It is a leadership issue and the chief executive must set the example."
> ~ Edward Hennessy ~

Leaders need to build and maintain the trust of people they lead and to this end, leaders must be honest; they must be in the habit of telling the truth consistently.

As leaders, we must be careful not to surround ourselves with advisers and audiences that only flatter our egos and never correct our missteps.

VALUE #2 Justice and Fairness

1. All the people you lead must experience unbiased and equal treatment, and must not feel justice is for some who may be your creditors, favourites, friends or family.

2. Great Christian leaders should rather be known as leaders who stand for the practice of justice than as leaders who use justice when it suits their own ends.

3. Let all people, even though they may not be pleased with the verdict or decision in a particular case or matter, feel they have been treated fairly.

4. We are counselled not to (1Co 4:5) "jump to conclusions with your judgments before all the evidence is in..."

5. Great leaders treat all people in an impartial, disinterested, detached and nonaligned manner, without prejudice, discrimination, prejudgement and intolerance.

6. When a certain person or group is critical of our leadership, we must be careful not to ill-treat, sideline or disadvantage the person or persons. Their criticism, which could be suspected to be from malice, may be stemming from their loyalty to you or to the cause, and their intentions may be to jealously guard you or the cause and not to break down.

In leadership, especially Christian leadership, we must learn to live cordially with and appreciate the critical and vocal opposition rather than to assume that the silence of the unspeaking majority means consent.

Leaders are better off with open critics than the kissing silent opponents whose resistance may be as subtle and dangerous as the proverbial Judas. Better an open and frank Peter than a kowtowing Iscariot. And here's the challenge for anyone who aspires to be a leader or serves as a leader; learning from Jesus, the Greatest Leader of all times; though He knew Judas' motives and intentions, He never treated him with slight, injustice and unfairness.

> "Justice discards party, friendship, kindred, and is therefore always represented as blind."
> ~ Joseph Addison ~
>
> Let all people, even though they may not be pleased with the verdict or decision in a particular case or matter, feel they have been treated fairly.

He lived out his inaugural axiom: (Mat 5:44) ".. When someone gives you a hard time, respond with the energies of prayer, (Mat 5:45) for then you are working out of your true selves, your God-created selves.

This is what God does. He gives his best--the sun to warm and the rain to nourish--to everyone, regardless: the good and the bad, the nice and the nasty."

7. Embrace all people under your leadership, as did President Barack Obama in his election victory speech, and President Nelson Mandela when he wore the Springbok jersey at the Rugby World Cup in 1995, (Khoza, 2006).

VALUE #3 Responsibility and Accountability

1. Hierarchal systems of governance have this fault in them, credit is taken by or given to the top person, but blame is shifted downwards. When all goes well, even without the effort and support of the CEO, or sometimes through the unilateral sweat and hard labour of the line person, praise goes to the one ultimately responsible for the organisation or department though he or she may have resisted the initiative.

2. In many instances those at the top reluctantly take responsibility for the failure of those they are leading. To save their skins, they work hard to expose their subordinates' actions whereas when there's credit, they tend to speak in plural and collective terms.

When the top leader presents a less than ideal report to the stakeholders and is criticised for it, there is some person or group of persons to blame in the hierarchy.

3. Great leaders receive the credit for their followers or subordinates when it comes, but are equally ready to personally and organisationally take the blame and responsibility when criticism is leveled at either the leader's performance or the subordinate's indiscretion or failure.

4. In leadership we must take collective responsibility for the good and the bad, the ugly and the beautiful. We need leaders who will take responsibility for their thoughts, words, attitudes and actions or inaction, not shifting the blame down the ladder when things go wrong.

5. On the other hand, the top leadership must be as accountable to the subordinates as they expect the subordinates or other members of the organization to be accountable.

Reports must be faithfully rendered by the MD, CEO or President as well as they are given by other directors and managers. Everybody must be regularly evaluated, appraised, encouraged, and corrected, when necessary.

> **We need leaders who will take responsibility for their thoughts, words, attitudes and actions or inaction, not shifting the blame down the ladder when things go wrong.**
>
> **In leadership we must take collective responsibility for the good and the bad, the ugly and the beautiful.**

This will ensure, among other things, growth, accountability and humility among all leaders.

6. Blanchard and Hodges suggest a small confidential group of two to seven leaders who meet regularly to "provide mutual support and accountability for continued growth and maturity in leadership as disciples of Christ..," (Blanchard & Hodges, 2005).

We need leaders who will take responsibility for their thoughts, words, attitudes and actions or inaction, not shifting the blame down the ladder when things go wrong.

7. We must learn to be each other's responsible and responsive keepers; keeping each other away from idleness, complacency, mediocrity, poor performance and ineffectiveness, and willing to listen to others' criticism of our actions, words and behaviour.

VALUE #4 Integrity and Commitment

1. Simplified, integrity is the ability of an individual, group or organization to think, act, live, and behave in consistence with its agreed, adopted or shared principles, values, beliefs and norms.

2. The opposite of integrity is hypocrisy, inconsistency, duplicity, and is probably best illustrated by Jesus' most direct and scathing attack on the theologians and scholars of his days (Mat 23:27) "'You're hopeless, you religion scholars and Pharisees! Frauds! You're like manicured grave plots, grass clipped and the flowers bright, but six feet down it's all rotting bones and worm-eaten flesh."

3. In this day and age when people say one thing and do another, Christian leaders must be people whose lives, actions, and attitudes are aligned with their values and beliefs.

4. It is fast becoming convenient, even in the Christian world, to think, act, behave and speak as everyone else, even in issues of leadership and human relations.

We treat each other with the same cruelty and derogatory ranking that we see in the world. Those in leadership positions look down upon those who are put under their care and leadership. This is passed down through the ranks and is perpetuated as a norm when in actual fact it is inconsistent with the Christian prescriptions.

While the organisational functions we perform may vary in degrees, salary scales and extent, our attitude and treatment of each other should not be that of bossing each other around.

We should treat each other with parity and as fellow leaders, (Mat 20:25-27) "So Jesus got them together to settle things down. He said, Let the senior among you become like the junior; let the leader act the part of the servant.' Paul, echoing the same thinking, says (Phi 2:5); "Think of yourselves the way Christ Jesus thought of himself. (Phi 2:6) He had equal status with God but didn't think so much of himself that he had to cling to the advantages of that status no matter what."

CALLED TO LEAD

> **In this day and age when people say one thing and do another, Christian leaders must be people whose lives, actions, and attitudes are aligned with their values and beliefs.**

5. As Christian leaders we must always endeavour to align our lives, our actions, our thoughts and attitudes with our beliefs, wherever we are, whatever we do.

6. Our commitment is to the Kingdom and its transformation in our lives and the lives of those we come across, those we lead and those we seek to influence towards God's agenda for their lives.

7. When our lives have not been in line with our beliefs or profession, we must confess, repent and right the wrong; seeking God's grace to become what are meant to be in our life's facets.

VALUE #5 Consistency and Goodness

1. As children we have been engaged in impromptu interaction where there were no rules of the game. We have felt angry and cheated when all of a sudden the leader of the game introduces the rules that were not known or agreed upon at the beginning of the game.

2. We all appreciate games that have rules of engagement that are consistently and equally applied to all of us.

3. Great leaders know the agreed rules and they play by the book. They do not insistently introduce new rules midstream the game or when they feel disadvantaged by the pending action or agreed rules of engagement. They subject themselves to democratic decision-making processes like any other person and refuse to bend the rules because they feel in a particular way about a particular point.

4. Great Christian leaders are driven by inner goodness and rules of fairness and they treat people consistently and with godliness.

5. Bad leaders are driven by evil, hidden agendas, personal convenience and changing ethics, and they inconvenience people and the organisations they lead with their ever changing rules of the game.

6. We must learn to apply the golden rule – do to others what you would like them to do to you.

7. Our leadership, especially as Christians, must not be characterised by the aggressive rule of the Darwinian jungle – do to others what they are likely to do to you, do it quickly and effectively before they do it to you. (Mat 12:35) "A good person produces good deeds and words season after season. An evil person is a blight on the orchard."

Great leaders know the agreed rules
and they play by the book.
They do not insistently introduce
new rules midstream the game or
when they feel disadvantaged
by the pending action or agreed
rules of engagement.

VALUE #6 Transparency and Openness

1. Those you lead must not feel, suspect and realise that you are conveniently hiding some things from them.

2. There must be no hidden agendas in your leadership as this will widen the gap in the trust between you as the leader and people you are called to lead.

3. When they say you are not transparent and you know they are right, come clean and repent.

4. Christian leaders must be open to other leaders as well as other people's thoughts on what needs to be done. No leader is an inexhaustible depository of ideas, thoughts and energy.

God has blessed each leader with a team that will support the leader's contribution, and any leader who is humble enough to listen to other people will not only be enriched by their insights but also energised through their active participation in the projects at hand.

5. Within an organization, leaders must trust other leaders' best interest, commitment and desire to see a cause or project carried on or finalised. Leaders will mutually benefit from opening up their hearts, hands and plans to each other.

Leaders who cannot trust other leaders stifle and eventually kill the work that needs to be done and they also delay the growth of fellow leaders so much that when the leader's time is up, there is no ready or groomed replacement.

6. Openness to criticism improves and freshens up that which would have remained stale and stagnant leadership contribution. "We all need truth-tellers, preferably those not directly impacted by what we do, who can help us keep on course. If you can't name any truth-teller in your life, or if you have avoided or undervalued the ones you have, it's time to change," (Blanchard & Hodges, 2005).

> There must be no hidden agendas in your leadership as this will widen the gap in the trust between you as the leader and people you are called to lead.

7. A leader who is open to criticism, debate, suggestions, and other people's ideas will grow and the organisation he or she leads will grow too. But a leader who is shut out from other people gradually isolates him or herself and hoards everything as his own, in the end prematurely aborts his or her leadership contribution.

"Too often in organisations, self-serving leaders cut off feedback by killing the messenger. Eventually the leader is fired, and although people had been available who could have given him or her helpful information, these leaders cut off the opportunity to grow... Bring truth-tellers in your life, they will tell you the truth if they know you will listen. It does not mean you have to do everything that they say, but they want to be heard," (ibid.)

(Ecc 4:9) "It's better to have a partner than go it alone. Share the work, share the wealth. (Ecc 4:10) And if one falls down, the other helps, But if there's no one to help, tough! (Ecc 4:11) Two in a bed warm each other. Alone, you shiver all night. (Ecc 4:12) By yourself you're unprotected. With a friend you can face the worst. Can you round up a third? A three-stranded rope isn't easily snapped."

VALUE #7 Self-Sacrificing Service

1. In stark contrast to the popular secular leadership praxis in which the leader is king or queen and the people are servants, great leaders elevate people to royalty and leaders see themselves as servants of the people.

2. In this subversive leadership, demonstrated, epitomised and promoted by Jesus Christ, the Greatest Leader our world has ever known, and approximated by other such great leaders as Moses, the second greatest leadership model, the leader is the server of the people. The leader comes to serve the people and is prepared to die for the people.

3. The people, their needs, salvation, redemption, liberation, their comfort and success are pivotal to the leader's mission and fulfilment. A server leader understands his or her mandate to be to live, and if needs be, to die for the vision, the people and the cause.

4. The leader voluntarily sets aside his personal interests, goals and popularity for the sake of the truth, vision and the people's joy. At the same time he or she is not a populist who seeks to rise to fame through making him or herself popular or by courting the love of common people.

Nonetheless, he or she has an unswerving commitment to serving people and he or she will do it even if he or she loses popularity. You may imprison this leader but you will never detain his or her commitment to service. You may crucify this kind of a leader but his or her crucifixion may just serve as service to humanity's needs.

5. A self-sacrificing leader spends his or her time thinking and implementing ways, systems and process by which he or she may effectively meet the needs of the people. The subversive server leader is consumed with the people's progress than his self-advancement and aggrandisement. This leader gives his or her life to serving people than in self-exaltation and demands for heroic service by the people.

6. The subversive server leader is less concerned about power and position, popularity and status, rights and entitlement, instead uses these to serve people not to demand service from them because of these privileges. His or her ultimate driving motivation is serving God, fulfilling his or her divine purpose of existence and bettering people's life.

Instead of demanding service from his or her people, he or she takes off his or her jacket to meet people's needs. He or she strips him or herself of his or her titles and status and gets dirty serving the people.

7. Instead of competition he or she seeks to cooperate with his or her teammates and even with his or her successors. In fact, he or she spends his or her energies, once the vision has been established, mentoring his or her team which will not only succeed him or her in the future but will multiply his or her efforts now. Power struggle is not part of the game.

The leader is not threatened by new or different talent; instead he or she manages and empowers the talent towards the perpetual progress and success of the cause now and in the future.

Called to Lead

When will you rise up, out of paralysing
apathy and desert seclusion?

When will you let your eyes sparkle with
hope, courage, and vision?

Arise, challenge and change the status quo for the better!

Untie all that binds and arrests humanity's
growth with any fetter!

Stand up and lead, that's your calling
from time immemorial!

Called to lead, called for now, called out of self-burial!

Human cries of despair!
Do they matter to you in this age?

Free them from the cage of meaninglessness
and start a new page!

Does human course or destiny concern you at all?

Rise up to make our world a better place for us all?

Come now, live for something,
live for someone and leave a legacy.

Novice Prayer†

Father, You know that this opportunity is something I am not looking forward to or excited about, yet here it is. Lord, help me see it as an opportunity to grow in endurance and grace and to be a witness of the strength that comes from You. Lord Jesus, help me find new meaning in what I am assigned to do.

Just as You learned and laboured in this world at a common trade, help me remember to do all things for the glory of God. Speak to my heart, plant a new song in my mouth, but most of all Father, teach me to trust You in the midst of this raging storm. I know that You will go before me, and in the dark night You will carry me. In You I put my trust. In Jesus's strong name, amen.

Apprentice Prayer†

Lord, this task seems harder than I thought it was. Maybe I'm not cut out to do it, but I know that You have faithfully brought me to this place and that You believe in me.

Help me to believe in myself, too! I want to do this assignment with the right heart and mind and to learn as much as I can, so remove my fears and false pride so that while learning, I can serve as well.

I want to demonstrate You to those around me, so calm my mind and help me do this well. In Jesus's name, amen!

Journeyman Prayer†

Lord, I don't know where to go from here. Because of some setbacks and mistakes I take responsibility for, I have lost my self-confidence and inspiration. I feel reluctant to step out of my comfort zone to teach others what I know or to act in a leadership position.

Lord, I know you have placed me here to be a light on a hill. Help me listen to wise counsel, be totally honest about my current situation, and be open to taking positive steps to the level of service and commitment I once enjoyed under Your wings of mercy and grace. In Jesus's name, amen!

Master/Teacher Prayer†

Lord, You know that I get tired and weary of teaching, leading, and serving those new to these tasks. I need Your strength, character and perseverance to do this again.

Help me see the reward in doing this because it is You that I serve. Let me nurture the enthusiasm of the novices and calm the fear of the apprentices.

Give me patience to respond with excitement to their questions and concerns. Let me not to reflect an unhappy but a heart that is full of love and compassion for each one of them and their situation.

Let the title "teacher" remind me of my own Master and Teacher – the Lord Jesus! In His name, amen!

† Ken Blanchard and Phil Hodges (2005)

Our High Calling

Regard every moment of time as golden.
Do not waste time in indolence;
Do not spend it in folly;
But grasp the higher treasures.

Cultivate the thoughts and expand the soul
By girding about the mind,
Not allowing it to be filled
With unimportant matters.

Secure every advantage within your reach
For strengthening the intellect.
Do not be satisfied with a low standard.
Do not rest content until by faithful endeavour,

Watchfulness, and earnest prayer,
You have secured the wisdom
That is from above.
Thus you may rise in character,

And gain influence over other minds
Enabling you to lead them
In the path of uprightness and holiness.
This is your privilege!

~ Ellen G White ~

PRAYER FOR LEADERS

Our dear God, who leads all everywhere, we thank you for those who follow the call to lead and redefine reality and rewrite human history. For those who take time to lift us up to greater heights than we have ever seen, thought or imagined.

We thank you for giving them the vision, talents, tenacity, inspiration, courage, faith, commitment and love. May their leading follow your ideals, always striving and approximating your agenda and purposes for humanity, transforming those they come into contact with to be like

You because they themselves will have been like You. O God, kindly strengthen their weak knees in times of discouragement and in the face of fear, adversity, challenges and resistance. Please sharpen and restore their vision when dim, dull or lost.

May our political, religious and business leaders be willing to serve at all times and circumstances; in season, out of season, in lush plains, and under dry and scotching desert sun, serving all they are sent to, irrespective of their genders, race, creed, education or status or ideologies.

May their commitment to the calling be as tenacious and relentless as it needs to, but ready to be replaced when called to pass it on to more energetic successors whose zeal and fervency will carry it faster and higher towards the pinnacle of Your eternal ideals.

May all leaders lead Your people with honesty, integrity, fairness and justice till we close all shores and enter the corridors of eternal reward and rest.

CALLED TO LEAD

FURTHER READING

1. Beers, R.A., Beers, V. G. & Rumford, D. 2004. Touchpoints For Leaders. Carol Stream: Tyndale House Publishers, Inc.

2. Blanchard, K. & Hodges, P. 2005. Lead Like Jesus. Nashville: W Publishing Group.

3. Peterson, E. & Southern, D. 2007. The Message of Leadership. Colorado Springs: NavPress.

4. Tutsch, C. 2008. Ellen White on Leadership. Nampa: Pacific Press Publishing Association.

5. Smalling, R. 2005. Christian Leadership. www.smallings.com

6. Khoza, R. J. 2006. Let Africa Lead. Johannesburg: Vezubuntu Publishing.

7. Maxwell, J. C. 2007. The Maxwell Leadership Bible. Nashville: Thomas Nelson, Inc.

www.ingramcontent.com/pod-product-compliance
Lightning Source LLC
Chambersburg PA
CBHW040458240426
43665CB00039B/78